Praying Up a Storm

Praying Up a Storm

Daniel Bernard

© Copyright 2004 – Daniel Bernard

All rights reserved. This book is protected by the copyright laws of the United States of America. This book may not be copied or reprinted for commercial gain or profit. The use of short quotations or occasional page copying for personal or group study is permitted and encouraged. Permission will be granted upon request. Unless otherwise identified, Scripture quotations are from the King James Version of the Bible. Scriptures marked NAS, NIV, and NKJ are from the New American Standard Version, New International Version, and New King James Version, respectively. Please note that Destiny Image's publishing style capitalizes certain pronouns in Scripture that refer to the Father, Son, and Holy Spirit, and may differ from some Bible publishers' styles.

Take note that the name satan and related names are not capitalized. We choose not to acknowledge him, even to the point of violating grammatical rules.

Treasure House

An Imprint of
Destiny Image® Publishers, Inc.
P.O. Box 310
Shippensburg, PA 17257-0310

"For where your treasure is, there will your heart be also."
Matthew 6:21

ISBN 0-7684-2962-5

For Worldwide Distribution
Printed in the U.S.A.

1 2 3 4 5 6 7 8 9 10 / 09 08 07 06 05 04

This book and all other Destiny Image, Revival Press, MercyPlace, Fresh Bread, Destiny Image Fiction, and Treasure House books are available at Christian bookstores and distributors worldwide.

For a U.S. bookstore nearest you, call
1-800-722-6774.

For more information on foreign distributors, call
717-532-3040.

Or reach us on the Internet:
www.destinyimage.com

Dedication

I dedicate this book to the many faithful intercessors in Tampa Bay, who have prayed long, hard, and in obscurity: especially, Karin Williams, Lynsey Klein, Anne Dew, Flo Warrington, Maria Carlton, Leslie Miller, Linda Green, Candy Spann, Gail Henderson, Betty Carter-Young, Bill and Pam Malone, Rev. Joe Brown, Pastor Ken Klassen, and the late Betty Ringer.

These prayer warriors have been some of the instruments God has used to pray His will for the Church in Tampa Bay. They also prayed for God's favor and hedge of protection around me and my family as we sought to unify the Church to glorify Jesus Christ our Lord.

Acknowledgments

Thanks to the many pastors in greater Tampa Bay who have come together in their respective geographical areas to pray and marshall their members to do the same. Their efforts are making this teaching more of a reality every day.

Thanks to Roy Jaeger, President of Associated Computer Services, who has lent his staff and equipment to work on this book. Special thanks to Kathy Bryant-George for her endless, selfless hours of editing and retyping.

Thanks to my wife, Kathy, who through home-schooling our children Leah, Luke, Bethany, Faith, Peter, and Rachel, inspired this teaching. I give praise to our Lord Jesus, Maker of the Heavens and the earth, who has showered me with His love and abundant blessings. All credit is due God the Holy Spirit, who revealed to me the teachings within these pages.

Endorsements

The storms of judgment and the storms of revival are coming face-to-face. The Church must use its God-ordained responsibility to take advantage of the season in which we live. *Praying Up a Storm* provokes and encourages us to be a part of revival rather than sitting back and watching lost and hurting people perish in the storms of judgment.

Doug Stringer
President, Somebody Cares America

Daniel Bernard has earned the authority to speak on this subject because of the cutting-edge work God has done through him and Somebody Cares Tampa Bay. Dan's example of a heart running hard after God, coupled with a deep compassion for hurting individuals, has left him standing among leaders across this nation and beyond. He's "doing the stuff."

Alice Patterson
Founder, Pray Texas

Daniel Bernard's book, *Praying Up a Storm*, brings a very important and timely message for the Church. We must repent, pray, and join together in unity for God to accomplish His will in our world today. Daniel brings new and fresh insight on Scriptures. We highly recommend this book and challenge you to not only read, but implement these teachings.

Bill and Pam Malone
Founders/Directors, Pray U.S.A.!

Daniel Bernard has tirelessly served the churches of his city for years, helping them pray toward Christ's glory with persistence and zeal. His dedication and vision are contagious. For some time he's been helping in other cities as well, in wonderful ways. He's always helped to stimulate united prayer focused on God bringing about a transformation of the entire community by the power of the gospel.

Steve Hawthorne
Director, WayMakers

If you desire to saturate your life and community with God's presence and power, *Praying Up a Storm* is a must read. Each page is filled with the passion the Holy Spirit has given Daniel Bernard to see every believer and the city in which they serve experience the supernatural outpouring of the latter rain necessary to reap the end-time harvest.

Pastor Paula White
Co-Pastor and Co-Founder
Without Walls, International Church

To every action there is a corresponding reaction. To every natural event, there is a spiritual event. Daniel Bernard has taken a natural, physical law and through a divine revelation has wonderfully drawn a spiritual law of the power of prayer ascending heavenward, creating a divine combustion and causing a heavenly release of God's glory to affect the course of man on the earth. Only men and women who have found the hidden power of prayer can write this kind of book. Caution…this is an action that will cause a great reaction!

Bishop Bart Pierce
Rock City Church

This book is a key from heaven on how to pray strategically for breakthrough to happen today. Daniel Bernard's *Praying Up a Storm* is fresh insight on how to walk in praying authority with a cutting edge. Daniel writes from experience, conviction, and a God-given mandate to call forth the church into intercession and prayer. *Praying Up a Storm* will quicken you to build up your prayer clouds in heaven to experience the "suddenly" of God!

Dr. Che Ahn
Senior Pastor, Harvest Rock Church

Table of Contents

	Foreword	13
Chapter 1	The Destiny of the Church Is at Hand	15
Chapter 2	The Prayer Cycle (Part 1)	23
Chapter 3	Persistent Prayer Fills the Clouds	33
Chapter 4	The Prayer Cycle (Part 2)	43
Chapter 5	Sins That Hinder	55
Chapter 6	Prayers That Overcome Hindering Sin	63
Chapter 7	Christ's Presence Over Your City	75
Chapter 8	Leaders Leading the Way to Revival	87
Chapter 9	God Breathes Through His Body	101
Chapter 10	Praying Up a Storm Means War	111
Chapter 11	Rain for the Nations	121
Chapter 12	A Canopy of God's Presence	133
	Study Guide	147
	Endnotes	167

Foreword

Daniel Bernard has one passion—that God's will be done on earth as it is in Heaven. To this end, Daniel labors with untiring focus. This book reflects this holy desire, especially in the practice of prayer. Prayer is God's idea to enable us to work with Him. We pray because God wants copartners in His Kingdom work on earth. *Praying Up a Storm* helps believers to bring the reign and rule of Jesus in lives and cities. This is a fresh message of repentance, unity, and prayer. The revelation found in these pages will convict you of the importance of prayer, help to heed God's call to pray for your city, and motivate you into your prayer closet. As a full-time prayer evangelist, I depend on tools like this to feed and nurture the prayer movement in the earth. Read it, study it, and become a better prayer practitioner.

Terry Teykl
Founder/President, Renewal Ministries

Chapter 1

The Destiny of the Church Is at Hand

DON'T FAKE THE FUNK ON PRAYER

Shaquille "Shaq" O'Neal, the center for basketball's Los Angeles Lakers, is physically amazing. He is 7'2" and over 300 pounds. In a television commercial, Shaquille is seen walking down the corridor of a basketball gym when he bumps into an invisible wall. Behind the wall is a former great center, Bill Russell of the Boston Celtics. Russell opens a peephole and says. "You're early." "I know," replies Shaq, "but I'm ready." "What's the password?" Russell asks. "Don't fake the funk on a nasty dunk," responds Shaq.

Let me interpret that for you. The team funk equals ability. In Shaquille's case, if you have the funk, or ability, to do a nasty dunk, you'd better not fake it; otherwise, you will have another seven-foot-tall phenomenon stuff the ball back in your face. If you have the ability to do the nasty dunk, you better come strong with it.

Shaquille passes through the imaginary wall and there stands two other Hall of Fame centers, Kareem Abdul-Jabbar and Bill Walton. Though they do not say a word, their presence implies this message,

"Shaquille, your destiny is the Hall of Fame. The key is, 'don't fake the funk on a nasty dunk.' "

Our destiny is to rule and reign with Christ. The presence of God prevailing in our churches and communities is God's will for us. Through prayer, we have the funk or the ability and authority given to us by Christ, but we have been faking it. As we pray, God will do a nasty dunk on the enemy. Our Omnipotent Savior, Jesus Christ, can dunk the devil anytime He wants. Yet, He has given us the privilege of joining Him in experiencing victory over our enemy, satan.

Hebrews 10:12-13 (NAS) states, "But He [Jesus], having offered one sacrifice for sins for all time, sat down at the right hand of God, waiting from that time onward until His enemies be made a footstool for His feet." In my opinion, Jesus is waiting for us to agree with Him and pray His Kindgom to come and His will to be done. Christ desires to rule nations, transform cities, and change lives.

Christ has given us the ability to do a nasty dunk on the devil. We have the ability to rule nations, transform cities, and change lives through the power of prayer. We can pray up the cloud of Christ's presence so He can pour out His Spirit. The Church's most glorious hour is set for fulfillment in our lifetime. The key to our fulfillment is this: Don't fake the funk on prayer for your city, nation, and world.

The Church reaches its destiny as it rescues lives. The Washington, D.C. snipers, who killed ten and wounded three, were caught through the power of prayer, and lives were rescued. Here's how it happened.

During the week of October 21, 2002, with the sniper at large in the Washington, D.C. area, 50 Christian truckers got together to pray that somehow the sniper would be caught. One of the truckers, Ron Lantz, who lived in another area, would be retiring as a driver in a few days, but he felt sure that God would answer their prayers. In fact, he told the others gathered there that God was going to use him to catch the sniper.

The Destiny of the Church Is at Hand

A few days later, Lantz was listening to the radio as he drove through the predawn darkness on Interstate 70 north of Washington, D.C. It was just a couple of miles from where the prayer meeting had taken place a few days earlier. As he slowly turned his rig and entered the rest stop parking area, he was shocked to see a car similar to the description he had just heard over the radio. He pulled over in front of it. Carefully trying to read the license plate by using his truck's headlights, a chill went up his back as the numbers matched! Lantz quickly called 911 on his cell, and following the directions of the police, pulled his truck across the exit for what he said were the longest 15 minutes of his life! There would be no escape for these elusive murderers. The rest is now history. The snipers were taken into custody without a shot fired.

Every day in our cities there are murderers, rapists, and other criminals, along with the missing adult and child victims, who need compassionate prayer, asking for the predators to be stopped and with them further tragedy to the victims. Behind these assailants is the evil one, whether they know it or not. Spiritually speaking there are thousands of demon snipers assigned to congregations and our cities. The enemy and his snipers seek to pick off people one at a time. Even though satan targets leaders both in and outside the Church, those who are actually picked off are done so at random.

Much like the D.C. snipers, satan and his demons are also random snipers. The snipers pick victims at random who are the most accessible or easy prey. The apostle Peter tells us of satan's strategy. In First Peter 5:8 he writes that the adversary is like a "roaring lion…seeking whom he may devour." The enemy picks off those who can be devoured or who are the easiest prey. The Church reaches its destiny by making it hard for people to be devoured in their cities. We do that by praying God's protection for those easily devoured, that they would come to know Christ and His protective and powerful presence. As we thwart the plans of demon snipers and rescue those who would be otherwise devoured, the Church builds an army of Christ warriors and marches on to its destiny. The army is growing at a miraculous rate.

Praying Up a STORM

THE LATTER RAIN IS AT HAND!

If God were to instigate a worldwide prayer movement we would know about it in His Word, because He does nothing until He has spoken to the prophets. Today, there is such a worldwide prayer movement, and God has foretold of it in His Word through His prophets.

> *For from the rising of the sun even unto the going down of the same My name shall be great among the Gentiles; and in every place incense shall be offered unto My name, and a pure offering: for My name shall be great among the heathen, saith the Lord of Hosts* (Malachi 1:11).

Malachi rebukes the priests who refuse to honor God and, in fact, dishonor Him by sacrificing blemished animals. God lets them know that whether they honor Him or not, He will be honored even among the heathen. Then a curious statement is made, "…and in every place incense shall be offered unto My name." This must have been a puzzling statement to the priests because only they offered up the incense and only in one place, the temple. The question is, "How is incense going to be offered in every place? Will many temples be established with an increased number of priests?" Yes.

The believers in Jesus Christ are the new priesthood (see 1 Pet. 2:9). We are the temple(s) of the Holy Spirit (see 1 Cor. 3:16). The incense we offer up is prayer (see Ps. 141:2, Rev. 8:3-4).

The following passage further illustrates the above teaching. Revelation 5:8-10 is the fulfillment of Malachi 1:11 and we, the Church of Jesus Christ on earth today, are those fulfilling this prophecy as we pray.

> *When He had taken the book, the four living creatures and the twenty-four elders fell down before the Lamb, each one holding a harp and golden bowls full of incense, which are the prayers of the saints. And they sang a new song, saying, "Worthy are You*

> *to take the book and to break its seals; for You were slain, and purchased for God with Your blood men from every tribe and tongue and people and nation. You have made them to be a kingdom and priests to our God; and they will reign upon the earth"* (Revelation 5:8-10 NAS).

The "bowls of incense" are the prayers of the saints (v. 8). We, His saints, who have been purchased by the blood of the Lamb unto God, are from every kindred and tongue, people and nation. All of us make up a kingdom of priests who shall reign on the earth. We are the priests redeemed by the blood of Jesus from every tribe and nation lifting up intercession so that His name will be great among the Gentiles.

Within these two passages, the promise of God's name being great among the heathen is foretold and fulfilled. The means by which it is fulfilled is through the worldwide prayer of His people.

PRAYING IN THE LATTER RAIN TO REAP THE END-TIME HARVEST

Another Scripture that refers not only to a worldwide prayer movement, but to a global harvest, is Zechariah 8:20-23:

> *Thus saith the Lord of hosts; It shall yet come to pass, that there shall come people, and the inhabitants of many cities: and the inhabitants of one city shall go to another, saying, Let us go speedily to pray before the Lord, and to seek the Lord of hosts: I will go also. Yea, many people and strong nations shall come to seek the Lord of hosts in Jerusalem, and to pray before the Lord. Thus saith the Lord of hosts; In those days it shall come to pass, that ten men shall take hold out of all languages of the nations, even shall take hold of the skirt of Him that is a Jew, saying, We will go with you: for we have heard that God is with you.*

Notice this revival is one of prayer. The inhabitants of one city shall go to another to pray and seek the Lord of hosts. It mushrooms from city to city, to people groups and nations (v. 22). They are moved by the Lord of hosts to "pray before the Lord."

Then note what takes place in verse 23: "Ten men shall take hold out of all languages of the nations, even shall take hold of the skirt of Him that is a Jew saying, We will go with you: for we have heard that God is with you."

The number ten represents completeness. Once we get to ten we start a new unit. Ten represents all the nations. "All nations shall take hold of the skirt of Him that is a Jew...."

This Jew, who the nations of the world are taking hold of, is Jesus. It is the Jesus they find in every true believer, every man who has been given His robe (or skirt) of righteousness in exchange for his own righteousness, which is as filthy rags.

Observe from Zechariah 8 that prayer precedes a global harvest. It is reported that over 170 million believers have been mobilized to pray for the salvation of souls and the unreached peoples of our world.[1] Intercessors are praying daily for souls, ministries, and nations. In response to those prayers, thousands are being saved: 20,000 a day in Africa; 35,000 daily in Latin America; 28,000 every day are converted in communist China. More than 70 percent of the progress in world evangelization from the time of Christ until today has occurred in the last three years.[2]

Zechariah 10:1 tells us to, "Ask [for the] rain in the time of the latter rain." By these reports it is obvious the latter rain and end-time harvest is upon us. More now than ever, it is time to ask for the latter rain in order to bring in the end-time harvest. My interpretation of the "latter rain" is simply a great outpouring of God's Spirit, whereby His presence is manifested throughout the Church causing a great revival within, and a great harvest of souls, as people are attracted. Other terms have been used by the Church, such as *spiritual awakening, revival, visitation, renewal, transformation,* etc. For the purpose of this book, we will most often use the term, *latter rain*, with the aforementioned definition in mind.

This teaching entitled, *Praying Up a Storm,* focuses on how the water cycle is a physical representation of what happens when we pray. In other words, the natural water cycle represents the reality of the spiritual prayer cycle. By revealing how the prayer cycle works, I hope to motivate us to pray in the latter rain to reap the end-time harvest.

CAUTION:

I am not proposing another formula to be used as a magic wand we wave to which God must respond. You may not even buy into the parallel between the water cycle and a prayer cycle. However, as you read, I pray that you will be stirred to a greater faith in our majestic, loving, compassionate God who desires to intervene and reign in the lives of individuals, cities, and nations. This faith should move you to believing prayer. If that takes place, then the purpose for which God moved on me to write this book has been accomplished.

Chapter 2

The Prayer Cycle (Part 1)

THE ELEMENTS

Where there is a physical law we can usually find a parallel or corresponding spiritual law. For example, the law of gravity can be likened to the law of sin and death (see Rom. 8:2). Both laws hold or pull things and people down. Of course, the law that causes one to defy the law of gravity is the law of aerodynamics. As long as birds and planes comply with the law of aerodynamics, they will overcome the law of gravity and fly. In the same way, as the Christian applies the law of the Spirit of life in Christ Jesus, he will soar victoriously over the law of sin and death. Another parallel of natural law and spiritual law is that of the water cycle to the prayer cycle.

The first two necessary elements in the water cycle are water and sun. Energy from the sun provides the heat, which causes evaporation, or vapor. As the sun warms the water, water molecules move faster and begin to bounce. Molecules far beneath the water's surface bump the molecules on the surface. These molecules escape into the air, becoming vapor.

GOD, THE SON

All prayer begins and ends with God. God is represented in the sun and water. God, the Son, the light of the world draws us to pray. Each of us has experienced the warmth of the Son of God urging us to commune with Him daily. As Jesus shines into our lives, the Living Water who is the Holy Spirit begins to move us to pray.

> *Who is he that condemneth? It is Christ that died, yea rather, that is risen again, who is even at the right hand of God, who also maketh intercession for us* (Romans 8:34).

Christ is seated on His heavenly throne making intercession for us. I believe Christ is praying our hearts would be moved to pray, because God has purposely limited His work on earth to His people, specifically to the prayers of His people. As E.M. Bounds states:

> When God declares that "the eyes of the Lord run to and fro throughout the whole earth, to show Himself strong in the behalf of them whose heart is perfect toward Him" (2 Chronicles 16:9), He declares the necessity of men. He acknowledges His dependence on them as a channel through which He can exert His power upon the world.[3]

GOD, THE HOLY SPIRIT

Water is a necessary component to cause vapors to ascend, beginning the water cycle; so it is with prayer. The Living Water, the Holy

The Prayer Cycle (Part 1)

Spirit, flowing in us as a river (see Jn. 7:37-39), is necessary for prayer. Mind you, this is not only for prayer to be effective, but I believe, for true prayer to happen. It is interesting to note that after Jesus gives the formula on how to pray in Luke chapter 11, He concludes the subject by saying, "If ye then, being evil, know how to give good gifts unto your children: how much more shall your heavenly Father give the Holy Spirit to them that ask Him?" (Luke 11:13)

It seems that Jesus not only gives them the formula for prayer, but also the Enabler of Prayer, the Holy Spirit. The scriptures reveal the Holy Spirit's role in prayer, the first being that of Instigator (see Acts 1:2,14). Zechariah 12:10 calls the Holy Spirit "the spirit of grace and of supplications." Grace is not only unmerited favor, but also God's power and ability. To paraphrase Zechariah 12:10, one might describe the Holy Spirit as the Spirit of power to pray.

By His power and ability, respond to the gentle nudges that come from the Son and the Holy Spirit to pray. Lift up your thoughts before the Lord. It is not necessary to always pray aloud; however, do so when you can. Prayer is communion with God from your heart and mind. As God impresses you, respond in prayer. This is how we pray without ceasing.

Smith Wigglesworth is a case in point of praying without ceasing and being obedient to the Lord's prompting to pray. It is told that Wigglesworth never prayed for more than ten minutes. However, it is said there was rarely a time when ten minutes went by that he was not praying.

The prayer life of Jesus has been extensively recorded. *After documenting the prayer life of Jesus, one concludes that He did not have a prayer life, but a life of prayer.* Jesus is the supreme example of unceasing prayer.

JESUS IS THE SUPREME EXAMPLE OF UNCEASING PRAYER.

I recently saw a church sign that communicated this truth. It asked, "If God were to call you, would He get a busy signal?" The lines of communication known as our spiritual hearts and minds need to be open, because God is calling moment by moment.

THE VAPORS

Jeremiah 10:13 states, "He [God] causes the vapors to ascend" (NKJ). Likewise, God the Son and the Holy Spirit working through us cause the prayers to ascend. (The vapor represents prayer.)

First Kings 8:10-12 will give us another type of this reality. The priests worshipped and prayed to God during the dedication of the temple. During the dedication, they used censers to burn incense. The incense also represents ascending prayers. (See Psalm 141:2, Revelation 5:8-10; 8:3-4.) This day the incense formed a cloud, and God filled the cloud with His very presence. The glory from His presence was so bright the priests could not stand to minister any further.

Of course, today we the Church are the priesthood that offers the incense in the form of prayer to God. Just as incense was a physical manifestation of a spiritual reality, so are the water vapors. Just as God causes every water molecule to ascend as vapor, He causes every prayer stated to ascend.

THE ROLE OF FAITH

Faith is necessary at this juncture. God answers prayers of faith. We cannot actually see the vapors ascending, yet we all know and believe they ascend because, ultimately, clouds do form and bring rain. Likewise, prayers ascending before God's throne cannot be seen with the naked eye. "Now faith is the assurance of things hoped for, the conviction of things not seen" (Hebrews 11:1 NAS).

It takes faith to pray up a storm. It takes faith in God that He is hearing your prayers and they are ascending before the throne of God.

We have already noted that God, the Son and Holy Spirit, initiate the prayer process just as the sun and water cause the vapor to ascend. As the vapor eventually makes clouds, so our prayers make spiritual clouds of God's will and presence over our lives. Faith is

The Prayer Cycle (Part 1)

nothing more than acting upon God's facts or Word. The water cycle is a physical law. The prayer cycle is no less a reality. In fact, it is more of a reality because our prayer cycle can supernaturally affect or supersede the water cycle. The message then is act on the facts. Act on the Word and pray, believing that just as God causes the vapors to ascend in order to form clouds and rain, He will do so spiritually to bring in the latter rain.

James 5:17-18 states, "[Elijah] was a man subject to like passions as we are, and he prayed earnestly that it might not rain: and it rained not on the earth by the space of three years and six months. And he prayed again, and the heaven gave rain, and the earth brought forth her fruit." Elijah was just like us, an ordinary person; but when he prayed by faith, it stopped raining for three and a half years. By faith he prayed again and it rained. We, as ordinary folks, avail before God as we pray and Almighty God avails on the earth on our behalf and on behalf of His Kingdom of which we are members. Everyday believers can pray up a storm. We can cause a spiritual downpour on the earth.

I was visiting a pastor friend of mine, Bill Traylor, in Texas. We were riding in his truck when a foreign voice came over his CB radio. "Pastor Bill, are you there, man?" a Jamaican voice asked. They had a short conversation, and afterwards I asked how he came to know the Jamaican man. "Well, I only know him through the radio," he said. I was surprised that the man didn't live nearby and was actually calling from Jamaica. "How can this little car CB radio reach Jamaica?" I asked. Bill explained that the Jamaican had a big megawatt unit that enabled him to communicate across thousands of miles of land, the Atlantic Ocean, and the Gulf of Mexico.

We are just one small unit, person, or congregation, but our effectiveness is not determined by how big we are or how many there are of us. We are hooked up to the big CB in the sky, Jesus, who lives to make intercession for us and desires to reach cities and nations.

Faith is praying for rain when there are no clouds in sight. Spiritually speaking, it means praying for God's presence when the spiritual atmosphere looks grim. Faith moves God.

Essential to faith is our willingness to step out in advance of an answer. John Bisagno, former Pastor of First Baptist Church in Houston, Texas, shares a touching story that illustrates this point. His five-year-old daughter came to him one day requesting a dollhouse. According to Pastor Bisagno, "I promised to build one and went back to reading an engrossing book. Soon I glanced out of the study window and saw my daughter with her arms filled with dishes, toys, and dolls, making her pilgrimage to the corner of the yard, where by now she had gathered a great pile of playthings. I asked my wife what the purpose of that impossible pile could be. 'Oh, you promised her a dollhouse,' she replied, 'and she believes you. She's just getting ready for it.' " It is not hard to imagine how quickly the father went to the task of building that dollhouse. Says the author, "I threw the book aside, raced to the lumberyard for supplies, and quickly built the little girl a dollhouse."[4] Similarly, God is moved by our faith. Unlike Pastor Bisagno, God is attentive and looking for those who will pray with faith to see God's Kingdom built.

FORMING THE CLOUDS

God is also moved to form the clouds of Christ's presence by our prayers of faith.

> *Ask ye of the Lord rain in the time of the latter rain; so the Lord shall make bright clouds, and give them showers of rain, to every one grass in the field* (Zechariah 10:1).

The clouds represent the presence of God. In First Kings 8:12, after the glory of the Lord filled the temple, King Solomon commented, "The Lord has said that he would dwell in the thick cloud" (NAS). Throughout God's word, a cloud represents God's presence.

The Prayer Cycle (Part 1)

Even the psalmist concurs when describing God in Psalm 97:2, "Clouds and darkness are round about Him; righteousness and judgment are the habitation of His throne."

The children of Israel were led by a pillar of cloud. This same pillar rested at the entrance of the tent of meeting each time Moses entered (see Ex. 33:9). A cloud of glory covered the top of Mount Sinai where God spoke to Moses and gave him the commandments (see Ex. 24:12-18; 34:5).

Clouds were also present in the life of Christ:

- At His transfiguration (see Mt. 17:5).
- At His crucifixion, the sky darkened (see Mt. 27:45).
- At His ascension into the clouds (see Acts 1:9).
- He now sits on a white cloud (see Rev. 14:14).
- He will return on the clouds (see Mt. 24:30).
- At the rapture in the clouds (see 1 Thess. 4:17).

CHRIST MAKES THE CLOUDS

...the Lord shall make bright clouds... (Zechariah 10:1).

And He that searcheth the hearts knoweth what is the mind of the Spirit, because He maketh intercession for the saints according to the will of God (Romans 8:27).

Again let me stress that God makes the cloud. He takes our prayers and forms them into His perfect will. The "He" referred to in Romans 8:27, I believe, is Jesus Christ, because the Bible states He is the one who knows and searches men's hearts. Jesus knew men's hearts while on the earth (see Jn. 2:24); and, in Revelation 2:23, Jesus speaks of Himself, saying, "I am He which searcheth the reins and hearts." In agreement with Romans 8:27 and 34, Hebrews 7:25 says that *Christ lives to make intercession as the great High Priest on our behalf.* As we pray, Jesus joins us in our intercession and begins to make the cloud of His presence according to the will of God. He forms a cloud of God's perfect will over our lives, churches, communities, and nations.

The churches in Revelation were consistently told, "He that hath an ear, let him hear what the Spirit saith unto the churches." As we hear what God's purpose and plan is for the local body and individual members and begin to send up prayers, Jesus takes them and perfects a cloud of His presence and a will for that situation and people.

As we "seek the Lord of hosts," we will be conformed into His likeness. As God purifies our hearts, our hearing will be finely tuned and our prayers will be more perfectly aligned with God's will (see 1 Jn. 3:2-3; Matt. 5:8)

Notice that, as Christ addressed each of the churches in Revelation, He gave each of them a promise. Though many of them had sinned, God gave them a hope and a future. We also need to pray the promises, not the problems. Daniel prayed in the promise of God found in Jeremiah's writing where it was foretold that after 70 years of exile, the Jews would return to Jerusalem.

However, the fact that God promised it did not make it automatic. The promises are not the possession. The promises are there for the possessing. The Israelites were promised the Promised Land. However, the group of Israelites to whom the promise was directly given did not possess the land because of disobedience. Also, remember that before Christ ascended He told the disciples to "wait for the promise of the Father" (Acts 1:4). Of course, Christ foretold of this promise in John's Gospel, chapters 14–16. But, as Peter told the crowd on Pentecost, the phenomenon which was presently happening had been spoken by the prophet Joel. This prophecy also was a promise. What did the apostles and others do to see the promise possessed? They waited and prayed for 40 days in Jerusalem.

The Prayer Cycle (Part 1)

Commenting on this subject, Brother Andrew writes:

> God's prophetic will, no matter how clearly set forth in the scripture, cannot happen until His conditions are met. Not everything goes according to the plan of God. The repeated apostasies of Israel were not God's plan. And the lawlessness of our own country is not God's plan.

God gave His only begotten Son, the most crucial aspect of His plan. Why, then, do not all subsequent events go according to God's plan? Because God is looking for intercessors for the world.[5]

PRAY THE PROMISES, NOT THE PROBLEM

The promises are God's plan. Pray them until they are possessed, until God rains down the manifested promise. We might say as Solomon:

> *Blessed be the Lord, that hath given rest unto His people Israel, according to all that He promised: there hath not failed one word of all His good promise, which He promised by the hand of Moses His servant* (1 Kings 8:56).

Each promise in God's Word is a by-product of who God is. The promise to meet our physical needs is based on the Lord as Jehovah-Jireh, God our Provider; the promise of healing on Jehovah Rapha, etc. Let me encourage you to "hallow His name" or set apart and make holy His name(s) as you pray. As you do so, you expand in your heart and mind how great and sovereign He is. We pray first and foremost because we love the privilege of a relationship with the Creator and Ruler of the Universe. In other words, we pray because He is God, our Creator and we are His creations; because He is our Father and we are His children; because He is our Redeemer and we are the redeemed. Yet, who He is, represents what He will do and wants to do for us and in us so that we will go forth proclaiming Him. Therefore, as you become familiar with the covenant names of God, worship and pray the covenant promises.

The God who makes and keeps covenant will not fail. I heard one preacher say, "I Am says, 'I will. If I do not, I am not I Am.'" If we will not give up "I Am" will show up.

This Old Testament strategy teaches us to war against the enemy by faith in God and praying His covenant promises. Filling up the cloud of Christ's presence by praying in His promises is a weapon of warfare that looses the enemy's hold on our lives and communities.

CHAPTER 3

Persistent Prayer Fills the Clouds

After the clouds are formed we need to fill them. Ecclesiastes 11:3 states, "If the clouds be full of rain, they empty themselves upon the earth." Zechariah 10:1 again says, "…the Lord shall make bright clouds, and give them showers." Vapors form the cloud; succeeding vapors then fill the cloud. We call this condensation. When the condensation becomes too heavy for the cloud to hold, it breaks forth with rain on the earth.

As the cloud of God's presence is formed, we must fill it. Depending on the spiritual need, the time and depth of prayer will vary. Regardless of the situation, the key is to pray, filling the cloud until it bursts. Therefore, we must persevere in prayer. In his book *The God Chasers,* Tommy Tenney expresses his view of God's response to persistent prayer: "I believe that when the conglomerate prayers of God's people gather together and finally reach a crescendo of power, hunger, and intensity, it finally gets to be 'too much' for God to delay any longer. At that point He finally says, 'That's it. I won't wait any longer. It is time!' "[6]

Jesus, when speaking on prayer, most often noted the need to persevere in prayer. A literal translation of Matthew 7:7 would read, "Ask and keep asking and it shall be given unto you, seek and keep seeking and ye shall find, and to him that knocks and keeps knocking, it shall be opened." We can persevere in prayer until it rains because God honors praying for the latter rain. Latter rain prayers are those that have unselfish motives at their heart. They are prayers that seek the latter rain for two reasons: 1) for God to be glorified through His saints and 2) for souls to be harvested. Other instances of persistence in prayer are in Luke 18:1 and 21:36.

As I noted earlier, Elijah was a man of like passion as us. The Bible says Elijah was just another man, yet God used his prayers to change weather patterns for years. We are taught to pray until God releases us (until He says yes or no); but here we are to pray as Elijah did—until it rains. This does not always mean lengthy seasons of prayer. Samuel prayed that God would send rain and lightning, proving to Israel they had sinned when they had asked for a king (see 1 Sam. 12:17-18). God did so immediately.

We are praying up a storm that will bring in the latter rain and usher in the great end-time harvest and the return of our Lord Jesus. Our prayers are not so we can fill our own little bucket with God's showers of blessings. Rather, we pray for a global downpour of the Spirit's manifested presence, resulting in worldwide revival. As we are hooked up with Heaven, we have the ability to pray Heaven's will down to earth.

> AS WE ARE HOOKED UP WITH HEAVEN, WE HAVE THE ABILITY TO PRAY HEAVEN'S WILL DOWN TO EARTH.

One example of praying in Heaven's will for souls to be saved was told by Dick Eastman, president of Every Home for Christ. Several years ago a pastor's wife was asked the reason their congregation was having tremendous growth. Was it new evangelism training? Did they start a school? The pastor's wife replied, "We have some great people and very good programs for outreach. However, this is why I think we are experiencing growth. One night about 2:00 a.m., I reached over to put my arm around my husband and grabbed air. I got up to see if he was sick or if something was wrong. I heard this strange sound coming from the garage. It sounded like moaning, as if something or someone was in pain. As I looked into the garage, there was my husband wrapped in a blanket under a tool bench muttering, 'Give me souls, God. Give me souls.' " It's Heaven's will that we have complete victories here in earth.

Joash, king of Israel, approached the amazing prophet Elisha, on his deathbed. Joash was anxious over his enemy, the Arameans, and was seeking reassuring words of victory from the prophet.

Elisha told the king to take his bow and arrow, and laying his hands upon the king's hands, shot an arrow through the east window. Then Elisha declared, "The Lord's arrow of victory, even the arrow of victory over Aram; for you will defeat the Arameans at Aphek until you have destroyed them" (2 Kings 13:17 NAS).

Then Joash was told to take the arrows he had brought with him and strike the ground. King Joash struck the ground three times and stopped.

> *So the man of God* [Elisha] *was angry with him and said, "You should have struck five or six times, then you would have struck Aram until you would have destroyed it. But now you shall strike Aram only three times"* (2 Kings 13:19 NAS).

The victory was already declared. Now it was Joash's turn to match or come into agreement with Heaven's will declared by Elisha. While Elisha was on his deathbed, he didn't have a desire to say goodbye to friends and family or make sure his estate was intact. He had one desire—to see the Lord's enemies vanquished. However, Joash didn't get the full intentions of Heaven, and Elisha was angry at Joash's apathy and lack of intensity.

You will read that God's desire is to give us the latter rain. You will discover it is there for the asking. But we, like Joash, have been apathetic and lacking intensity. How long will it take and how much prayer will it require? I don't know. This is why you walk by faith and not by sight. God has promised it. The question is how bad do you want it?

Some YMCAs have an acrostic on their gymnasium walls that tells how one can get physically fit:

Frequency

Intensity

Time

The amount of prayer needed to transform our cities will vary. There is no set formula for getting the Church and our cities spiritually fit. However, we do know it will take frequency of prayer, with much intensity, over time. Praying frequently, with intensity, over time will not only cause revival, but will also make us fit or ready to be recipients of revival of God's presence over our cities.

FILL THEM WITH ALL KINDS OF PRAYER

Clouds are to be filled up with all kinds of prayers. They are to be prayers that are not only intercession and supplication, but also praises to God for who He is and thanksgiving for what He has done and will do. Therefore, as we praise and thank God for being Jehovah Jireh, we are demonstrating faith in Him to manifest Himself that way on the earth. Evangelism is revealing God for who He is so that people will come to know Him. As we fill up the cloud with praises of who God is and what He's done, we can expect to see Him manifested on the earth according to our prayer.

Francis Frangipane stated that the key to victory is Christ seated in the heavenly places. As the praises of God ascend, it develops the cloud of Christ's presence in the heavenly places. Where Christ is, the devil must flee. As the psalmist said, "Yet You are holy, O You who are enthroned upon the praises of Israel" (Ps. 22:3 NAS). As the praises go up, the cloud of Christ's presence moves in; as was the case in the dedication of the temple found in Second Chronicles 5:13-14:

> *It came even to pass, as the trumpeters and singers were as one, to make one sound to be heard in praising and thanking the Lord; and when they lifted up their voice with the trumpets and cymbals and instruments of music, and praised the Lord, saying, For He is good; for His mercy endureth for ever: that then the house was filled*

with a cloud, even the house of the Lord; so that the priests could not stand to minister by reason of the cloud: for the glory of the Lord had filled the house of God.

This Scripture illustrates how, through praise, the cloud of Christ's presence is not only made but filled. Remember, satan is a glory hog and cannot stand the praises offered unto God. As Christ's presence is ushered in through praise, satan flees.

In First Corinthians 10:1-2, Paul refers to the Israelites being baptized in the sea and in the cloud. These baptisms are types representing water and Spirit baptism. I believe the reason we are baptized in the cloud (see 1 Cor. 10:1-2) is so we can pray in the Spirit with all kinds of prayers and supplications (see Eph. 6:18).

When we say "all kinds of prayers," it also means praying in the Holy Spirit. Even though we may not know what the will of God is, the Holy Spirit does and prays accordingly. Therefore, pray in the Holy Spirit by using an unknown prayer language. Although your church may not use this form of prayer, I share this for those whose tradition sees this as a valid scriptural form of prayer. Praying in the Spirit, in an unknown language or groanings, is another effective means of filling the cloud of Christ's presence. This type of praying transcends our understanding and knowledge. Therefore, as you pray in the Holy Spirit (prayer language), you are praying in the perfect will of God because the Holy Spirit has perfect union with the Father and Son.

Paul also encouraged the Corinthian brethren that they should pray to receive an interpretation of that tongue (see 1 Cor. 14:13). The interpretation is for the one praying and the Church (others who are also praying). Since you are praying the perfect will of God by praying in the Spirit, receiving an interpretation of what you are praying will give you the understanding of His perfect will and encourage you to pray more fervently.

As we pray in the Spirit, we must believe the Holy Spirit is praying the perfect will of God. As we then ask for interpretation, the Holy Spirit will speak to us what the will of God is. He will impart to us how to pray. We are then getting revelation from the Holy Spirit to pray strategically in the heavenly realms. As these things are revealed, our faith increases, as does the prayer. Thus the vapor forms the cloud of Christ's presence over a city, neighborhood, or community.

WHEN FASTING IS LIKE FEASTING

Jesus said, "Howbeit this kind goeth not out but by prayer and fasting" (Mt. 17:21). Jesus was specifically referring to the casting out of demons of a possessed individual. However, the principle of praying and fasting to see the devil removed and Christ's purpose and will prevail, can be applied here as well. Praying and fasting not only hasten the filling of the cloud of Christ's presence, but will cause the great cloud to burst. Additionally, a sign that revival is not far away is when fasting is as feasting. Zechariah 8 is a chapter on revival. In verse 19 of that revival chapter it says:

> *Thus saith the Lord of hosts; The fast of the fourth month, and the fast of the fifth, and the fast of the seventh, and the fast of the tenth, shall be to the house of Judah joy and gladness, and cheerful feasts; therefore love the truth and peace.*

The fasting by the house of Judah, by the people of God, in times of revival will be as joy and gladness and cheerful feasts. Our fasting will be as feasting because being in His presence will satisfy us just as it did Moses. Fasting will be as feasting because our spirits will be feeding on the powerful presence of the Lord Jesus Christ by the Holy Spirit.

> OUR FASTING WILL BE AS FEASTING BECAUSE BEING IN HIS PRESENCE WILL SATISFY US JUST AS IT DID MOSES.

A month or forty days of fasting seemed to be far-fetched even a few years ago; however, now it is a reality. The difference is the Lord of Hosts is moving across our land. The late Dr. Bill Bright, Evangelist Morris Cervlo, Steve Hawthorne, Max Lucado, Doug Stringer, and others are

Persistent Prayer Fills the Clouds

catalysts of the Holy Spirit in implementing forty-day periods of prayer and fasting taking place across the country.

Here is a contemporary example of how God responded in a mighty way to praying and fasting. Pastor Blake Lorenz of Pine Castle United Methodist Church in Orlando, Florida, was embroiled in a battle for the pastorate of the church. The two business meetings intended to resolve the issue brought greater division and spiritual depression out of the need to see God's fire fall.

Pastor Lorenz decided to call a 10 day fast. Recalling the days between Jesus' ascension and Pentecost, when the fire of the Holy Spirit fell from Heaven, they began. Pastor Lorenz explains how fasting and prayer changed the spiritual atmosphere and personal direction.

> The first night, we studied Exodus 33 and 34, in which Moses begged to experience God's presence. We observed Moses coming before God, head bowed to the ground, lying prostrate before him (34:8). We realized that a prostrate person is dead to self, vulnerable and pliable to God. We determined to get as low before God as we could.
>
> At the close of our time in the Word, the church body, especially the men, came to lay prostrate before God all around the altar. We lay there for quite a few minutes, utterly moved as we sought God with all of our hearts. The next night we continued studying the presence of God. We observed that when the people of God experienced God's presence in the wilderness, it was a physical presence, a pillar of fire at night or a cloud by day. God showed us that His presence is more than some abstract thought—it is a concrete experience.
>
> I then shared my testimony of when Jesus Christ had come into my bedroom more than two decades perviously. It had been as though the gates of heaven had opened so I could be right there in Jesus' presence.

I had experienced such agape love; I knew nothing in this world could hurt me. I had wanted to stay in His presence forever because of the absolute peace.

Suddenly, right in the middle of that testimony, the gates of heaven opened to me again. As I stood in front of my congregation, the Holy Spirit showed me that I had missed His calling on my life. When Jesus had come to me that night in 1980, it was to appoint me to call people into God's deeper presence. Yes, I had called people to repent and trust in Jesus Christ as Lord and Savior; but God wanted me to do that plus lead people to experience this deeper sense of His love and rest, just as I had that night.

Deeply moved, I told the people that I had just discovered my destiny. Someone yelled, "Preach it!" But I could not speak. God's presence and conviction overwhelmed me. For a few moments I stood silent with my eyes closed. I fell to my knees, then prostrate, weeping because I had allowed the world, self, and the church to keep me from God's call on my life. As I lay there God took something out of me. I felt it leave. As that happened, the same love and peace overwhelmed me as before. It was as though Jesus had walked past me and the hem of His garment had brushed the side of my face.

Without a word, people streamed to the altar to seek God's face and lay prostrate before Him. Soon the entire altar and stage area were filled. After a season of prayer, two of my leaders came and held up my arms like Aaron and Hur had for Moses during the battle with the Amalakites. I asked forgiveness for an event three years prior, and for becoming sidetracked from God's call. What a mighty time of prayer and victory!

The next eight days of our prayer and fasting were filled with a growing sense of God's presence. I received emails, notes, and phone calls telling how every night people were being healed physically, spiritually, and relationally....

From this time of prayer and fasting, God has given our church fresh vision. I was asked to continue on as pastor, and we are more united than ever before.[7]

God heard the cry of a desperate people. This example gives us hopeful expectation of how God wants to visit us with fresh rain from above. The rain of His presence will change the lives of individuals and Churches, and ultimately transform our communities.

Our fasting says to the Lord of Hosts, "Without You we are a dry, thirsty land. We need You to pour out Your latter rain to make us streams to our cities, which are spiritual deserts."

ALL KINDS OF PRAYER BY ALL KINDS OF PEOPLE

God uses everyday moms like Gail Henderson. Gail watched *A Charlie Brown Christmas* one night with her children and was moved by how these animated children had such an effect on her as they told the Christmas story.

She decided to use the children in her neighborhood to do their own Christmas pageant. Over 120 people came out to watch this neighborhood children's play. Several came to Christ through the presentations, including a Muslim neighbor. Soon she was sharing with others how to put on these Christmas pageants. From the pageants, she was led to help other women creatively pray and reach their neighbors. She is now the "love your neighbor coordinator" for the state of Florida. Gail has mobilized over 300 women who are actively praying for their neighbors in Tampa Bay.

LIVE PRAYER

Another example of people God uses is demonstrated through the life of Bill Keller and those he has mobilized. Raised in the United Methodist Church, Bill Keller felt a call to the ministry at a young age. However, starting a successful business while attending Ohio State altered the course of his life and his future. His success was soon lost after being convicted of insider trading of the stock market, and he spent two and one-half years in a federal prison. While in prison, Bill was able to find his way back to his faith and worked to receive his undergraduate degree in Biblical Studies from Liberty University of Lynchburg, Virginia.

Upon his release from prison, Bill went into full-time ministry and the door opened for him to work at TV-38, Chicago's Christian television station. By June 1993, Bill incorporated Bill Keller Ministries and then left TV-38 in early 1994 to devote all his time to his growing ministry. He started the first Christian 900 service, developed a corporate chaplaincy program, and held evangelistic meetings in downtown Chicago to impact the business community.

It was Monday, August 30, 1999 that proved to be the greatest adventure yet for Bill Keller. It was on this day that Liveprayer.com signed on the Internet becoming the first 24 hour–a-day, 7–day-a-week "LIVE" Internet broadcast. Now people worldwide could log on to the Internet anytime of the day or night and have someone pray for their needs.

Liveprayer.com has over 20,000 visitors daily to the website, 20 percent of which come from outside the United States. There are over 1,700,000 people who subscribe to the Daily Devotional written by Bill Keller and there are over 40,000 prayer requests received daily, to which a ministry team sends personalized responses.

There are reports of over 35,000 people who have accepted Christ as their personal Savior, at least 50 people who have chosen to live after contacting Liveprayer.com when on the verge of committing suicide, and over 900,000 praise reports from people who have requested prayer for many different reasons through Liveprayer.com. These needs could only be met through a supernatural move of God.

Bill works with retired pastors and other retirees all over the world in this incredible prayer force. What a terrific way to reinvest your life and see many people be transformed by the power of prayer and the gospel. God is not a respecter of persons. He will use anyone at any stage of life to rain down His blessings on the earth. Why not commit to be one of them?

Chapter 4

The Prayer Cycle (Part 2)

THE BLESSINGS COME DOWN

The rain represents answered prayer, and answered prayer is God intervening on the earth. Each time He intervenes, His presence and person is manifest.

Hosea 6:3 states, "He shall come unto us as the rain, as the latter and former rain unto the earth." Jesus will manifest Himself, raining down His very presence, and it will be displayed in our lives and situations. Jesus rains down Himself by the Holy Spirit. The latter rain, again, refers to a great outpouring of the presence and power by the Holy Spirit manifesting the presence of Christ.

> *Be glad then, ye children of Zion, and rejoice in the Lord your God: for He hath given you the former rain moderately, and He will cause to come down for you the rain, the former rain, and the latter rain in the first month....And it shall come to pass afterward, that I will pour out My spirit upon all flesh; and your sons and your daughters shall prophesy, your old men shall dream dreams, your young men shall see visions: and also upon the servants and upon the handmaids in those days will I pour out My spirit* (Joel 2:23,28-29).

Speaking prophetically, Joel tells how the Lord will come down in the former and latter rain. The former and latter rain foretold in verse 23 is later described in verses 28 and 29. These verses were quoted by Peter and the apostles as explanation of the miraculous outpouring of the Spirit that took place on the day of Pentecost in Acts 2. The manifestations of the Spirit in the infant stage of the Church were the moderate former rain, and we are now experiencing the greater latter rain.

GOD WILL RAIN DOWN HIS WORD

For as the rain cometh down, and the snow from heaven, and returneth not thither, but watereth the earth, and maketh it bring forth and bud, that it may give seed to the sower, and bread to the eater: so shall My word be that goeth forth out of My mouth: it shall not return unto Me void, but it shall accomplish that which I please, and it shall prosper in the thing whereto I sent it. For ye shall go out with joy, and be led forth with peace: the mountains and the hills shall break forth before you into singing, and all the trees of the field shall clap their hands (Isaiah 55:10-12).

Just as God waters the earth, causing it to be fruitful, God also rains down fresh revelation from His Word to cause our lives to be fruitful. What most of us need is wisdom and direction. If we only knew what God specifically wanted, we would do it. We would be in His will and, therefore, successful.

God is looking for people who have faith not just to go to Heaven, but also to bring Heaven down to earth. "Thy kingdom come. Thy will be done in earth, as it is in heaven" (Mt. 6:10). We need to pray in Heaven's will. His Kingdom means His rulership in the hearts and lives of those in our schools, communities, and neighborhoods. God manifests His

The Prayer Cycle (Part 2)

Word in the life of believers, which causes them to bring forth and bud or bear the fruit of Christ and prosper.

Notice Isaiah 55:11 states that God will accomplish that which He pleases or desires through His Word. He desires to accomplish His will and love into our hearts. He has plans to accomplish things for His Kingdom through us, and He wants to do immeasurably more than we could ask or imagine. Therefore, believe Him at His word. Pray up a storm that will bring the latter rain, and He will manifest His presence through His believers. His desire is to put the Kingdom of God within us in ever-increasing measure, so we will establish it on the earth.

From these passages in Isaiah, we see God's Spirit is going to manifest Himself in purity and power for Christ-like ministry and character. We will see the miraculous. We will see the supernatural ministry of Christ poured out on His Body worldwide. Equally, as God rains down His Word, we shall see Christ formed in us, giving the ministry credibility.

This word that we receive is the living *rhema* word of God. As God rains down His presence, the *logos*, or written Word, will become a *rhema* word. A word that we see from God's Word will have new depths of understanding. Old familiar passages will become new revelation in our lives.

Speaking of Israel's provision when in the wilderness, Psalm 78:23-24 states, "Though He had commanded the clouds from above, and opened the doors of heaven, and had rained down manna upon them to eat, and had given them of the corn of heaven."

As we pray and fill up the spiritual cloud, we can expect God will command it to open and rain down fresh manna or spiritual food found in His Word for His people.

God will also rain down prophetic words, such as this prophetic teaching God rained down into my mind and heart. There will also be true prophecy that will be specific, accurate, and consistent with God's Word, bringing us into a closer relationship with Jesus.

IT'S GOD'S DESIRE TO GIVE THE LATTER RAIN!

God desires to give the latter rain. According to Zechariah 10:1, it is there for the asking. First, God desires to give it in order to bring His people to maturity. Our lives, once matured, give God glory. James 5:7 states, that God gives the former and latter rain to bring forth "precious fruit." This term means, "complete, mature or ripened fruit." The ripened life means the believer is living like Christ. Just as the earth depends on the rain in order to produce its fruit, so is the Bride dependent upon Christ to pour out His Spirit so we might bear His fruit.

The second reason God wants to give the rain is for the end-time harvest. It is the latter rain, which brings forth "precious fruit" of Christ in us, making us the harvesters of the end-time harvest. "Neither say they in their heart, Let us now fear the Lord our God, that giveth rain, both the former and the latter, in His season: He reserveth unto us the appointed weeks of the harvest" (Jer. 5:24).

The purpose for the latter rain is the appointed end-time harvest. This is the reason we pray for the latter rain and why God will readily give it.

As God rains down His Word, it waters the souls of men on earth (see Isaiah 55:10-11). Then, budding with the fruit of the Spirit, they go out with joy and are led forth by peace (v. 12). As we receive the latter rain, we become joyful harvesters, fruitful, using the sickle, God's Word, to reap. This is what the phrase, "He gives seed to the sower and bread to the eater," can mean. As God rains down His Word in us, it becomes our seed to sow. As we sow that seed, it becomes the bread of eternal life, which the ravished unbelievers eat in order to never hunger again (see Jn. 6:48-63).

Ezekiel 47 is a chapter describing the river of life, which flows from God. This very river flows through us. As we receive the latter rain, we receive the river of Living Water, the Holy Spirit. We are His riverbed in which to flow. In verse 8, the river flows into the sea, healing the waters in the sea. Then, in verse 9, everything this river touches in the great sea will live and be healed. The sea represents many nations and peoples (the sea of humanity) (see Rev. 17:15). As we receive the latter rain, we become a river of life flowing into nations, tribes, and peoples, bringing healing and life through the gospel of our Lord Jesus Christ, reaping the harvest. The lyrics of Graham Kendrick's song, "Shine, Jesus, shine," agree. "Flow, river flow, flood the nations with grace and mercy...."

Finally, God desires to give the latter rain because it will mean the return of Christ for His Church. Jesus Christ desires to return for His own. He desires to have the long-awaited wedding feast with His Bride.

In James 5, the statement about the "precious fruit" wrought by the former and latter rain is sandwiched between two sentences about the coming of the Lord Jesus.

> *Be patient therefore, brethren, unto the coming of the Lord. Behold, the husbandman waiteth for the precious fruit of the earth, and hath long patience for it, until he receive the early and latter rain. Be ye also patient; establish your hearts: for the coming of the Lord draweth nigh* (James 5:7-8).

God gave the former rain to the apostles on Pentecost, which started the Church and its march to the end of time. The latter rain brings the Church and the Church Age to maturity and completion. Therefore, the term "precious fruit" specifically refers to the completion of the Church Age.

Jesus referred to the Father as the husbandman (see Jn. 15:1). The Father has patiently waited for this latter rain—the outpouring of the Holy Spirit to come. This outpouring produces the great end-time harvest of souls. The apostle Paul calls this the fullness of the Gentiles coming in (see Rom. 11:25), after which the husbandman, God, the Father, would send back His Son, Jesus Christ.

Only the Father, or the husbandman, knows the day or the hour of Christ's return (see Mt. 24:36). However, we can know the season. His coming will immediately follow the latter rain, which brings the final ingathering of souls. If we are experiencing the latter rain, then Christ's return is right around the corner! Hallelujah!

ISAIAH DESIRED THE MANIFEST PRESENCE

The expository preaching of Isaiah 64 by Dr. Bill Anderson, former pastor of Calvary Baptist Church in Clearwater, Florida, stirred my spirit and inspired the following thoughts.

Isaiah, the prophet, prayed and asked God to manifest Himself. Isaiah pleaded for God to open the heavens and come down, shake the mountains, bring fire, and make the water boil. In other words, Isaiah was saying, "God, we want Your presence to be tangibly seen." Why? Verse 2 tells us: "...to make Thy name known to thine adversaries, that the nations may tremble at Thy presence!"

Isaiah's desire for the manifest presence of God was not in order to boast of a spiritual experience, nor was it for Isaiah to be personally consoled or reassured; but rather to see Jehovah glorified and known among all peoples.

Isaiah, being a prophet of God, understood God was omnipresent. He was not satisfied with the mere knowledge that God was there. He desired God to show up in power to save the nations, even his own.

The people of his day needed to see the tangible presence of God. In Isaiah's eyes, power from Heaven would be necessary to awaken Israel and other nations to the reality of the Almighty God. What they needed is what we need today. At no other time on the face of the earth have we had such a myriad of cults, spiritual powers, worldly philosophies, and temptations drawing millions to eternal darkness. The spiritual war is coming to an apex. We will see and need more Mt. Carmel experiences in the days to come to bring light into the darkness that shadows our cities and nations.

We need saints, like Isaiah, who are not satisfied with the cloud of Christ's presence, but desire His manifest presence. If we have been the least timid before to ask the Lord to show up powerfully, let us throw it off completely now. Isaiah is proof. It is acceptable and even right to call upon God to rend the heavens and come down. Call upon Him to burst the cloud and pour out His latter rain.

Verse 4 (NAS) states that God is prepared to act for those who wait on Him. God is ready to act. Are you waiting? Could this be what is holding back our Lord? It appears that Heaven's silence was Israel's fault. Isaiah describes the problem in verse 7: "And there is none that calleth upon Thy name, that stirreth up himself to take hold of Thee...."

Israel was not waiting, stirring, or seeking to take hold of the God who was ready to act. Let it not be said the same of the Church of our land.

In verses 11 and 12, Isaiah laments over the ruined cities in Judah and Israel. He then asks, "Will You [God] keep silent...?" (NIV) Our compassion for our ruined cities and lost nations and our ineptness to save them should cause us to cry out for God's reticence to be broken and His might displayed. As we stir ourselves to take hold of our Lord, He will act! He will pour out His manifest presence and bring the awakening we need.

Isaiah asked God to shake the mountains as He had done before (see Ex. 19:18). Isaiah had a point of reference where God shook a nation by shaking a mountain. Our point of reference is Acts 4 where God shook His people who were shaking the world with the gospel. In that first-century church, Christ was not only present, but He was tangibly present by the Holy Spirit. Miracles were occurring in the marketplace, not just the temple.

GOD MANIFESTS A MIRACLE

One year, on July 3, while I was on my way home looking forward to celebrating my birthday on July 4, my wife called and said, "Go to All Children's Hospital; something has happened to Benjamin, our nephew. I don't know the extent of the injuries, but he had an accident on a jet ski in a nearby lake. Your brother didn't speak much; he just said it was bad and to come."

Praying Up a STORM

Arriving at the hospital, I found Benjamin was unconscious. He had crushed his skull in four places after he had accidentally gunned the jet ski close to an embankment. As the jet ski went airborne, landing on the ground, Benjamin was thrust off, his head hitting a tree stump, crushing his skull.

Making it through the night was a first priority. Because the incident was being broadcast on various news channels, many people saw our last name and called thinking Benjamin might be a relation to me. Prayer quickly spread throughout the Bay area for Benjamin. We continued to pray the healing promises from God's Word over him.

He made it through the night. The next step was for the swelling to go down so that hospital staff could do tests and evaluate the damage to his brain. When the tests were completed, the news was not good. After Benjamin had been in a coma for ten days, the doctors informed my brother, Norman, that there was little-to-no brain activity. If Benjamin ever did wake up, he would be a complete vegetable. "How about some of his movement of his body?" Norman questioned. "The movement is involuntary nerve reactions," the doctors explained.

Trials and testing have a way of building faith, which is what happened in my brother. He responded to the doctors, "Well, you don't have the last say; God does." The doctors just shrugged it off as a father in denial.

Shortly after the doctors had given the bad news to the family, Norman was with Benjamin when he suddenly woke up. Not only did he wake up, but he also started to talk. "I'm hungry," he said. For an 11-year-old boy to be hungry after ten days in a coma could have been considered a flex reaction. Then he said, "Hi, Dad!" When Norman asked him, "How old are you?" he slowly slurred, "Eleven." Norman then took a baseball and asked him what it was. He easily identified it.

The nurses quickly called one of the doctors who was on a plane, and shouted with excitement. Those unbelieving doctors said it was their first real miracle. Just three hours earlier, they had basically determined Benjamin to be brain dead. A year later you would have never known he had been in an accident.

I challenge you to boldly call upon God to manifest Himself in power, that He would be known not only in church buildings, but also among nations, in the marketplace, and even among His adversaries.

A NEVER-ENDING CYCLE

The prayer cycle is like the water cycle—it is unending. The water cycle is always in effect. The fact that it is not raining does not mean the cycle is not in operation. Vapors are going up, it will eventually rain, and it is always raining somewhere on earth. The Bible says to "pray without ceasing" (1 Thess. 5:17).

The difference in this cycle and the water cycle is that the prayer cycle is not limited to natural conditions. In other words, we petition God to rain upon us continually. He desires for us to live and enjoy His presence constantly. If we will pray and ask God for rain in the time of the latter rain, He will make bright clouds. We can experience daily new revelation, divine appointments, miraculous answers, and souls saved as a result of our prayers.

Our lives and communities can be a rain forest. The latter rain and spiritual blessings that come with it can be an ongoing experience, especially now, because now is the time of the latter rain and great harvest.

Dr. David Yonggi Cho's church in Seoul, Korea is a good example. They have 24-hour "prayer mountains" where people spend hours praying. These prayers have produced a church of one million, making it the largest in the world. They are also a group of dedicated harvesters sending missionaries to every continent.

THE PENSACOLA OUTPOURING

Another living example of this teaching is the Brownsville Assembly of God in Pensacola, Florida. Pastor John Kilpatrick was one who confronted sin head-on in his personal life and in his members' lives. From this holy life came a great yearning for revival. His hunger led him to establish Sunday evenings as a time for weekly prayer meetings. Banners were made to signify specific prayer points, which ranged from local church and community needs to national and international concerns. The prayer evenings grew in number and in length for years, and a spirit of revival was in the air. For many years, Brownsville Assembly prayed up and filled the cloud of Christ's presence over their body, if not Pensacola itself, until the rain began to fall on Father's Day, June 1995.

Brownsville met Wednesday through Sunday evenings for revival for 3 years. A reported 155,000 have been saved. The staff at the church was so overwhelmed that it was impossible to categorize the other various commitments. On Tuesday nights, they continued to fill up the cloud with 1,000 prayer warriors assembled to intercede. Throughout the week they had 40 full-time trained intercessors praying. On a citywide scale, Pensacola's crime rate has declined nearly 20 percent during that period of time. Brownsville Assembly currently maintains a Thursday night intercessory prayer gathering that averages 500 participants and a Friday night revival service.

Let me summarize by saying that what has happened in Pensacola is due to the Brownsville Assembly meeting the conditions for revival. I believe those conditions are: 1) zero tolerance for sin; 2) faith to pray for revival through a prophetic promise given by David Yonggi Cho of Seoul, Korea; 3) mobilizing the body to pray over the city, which ushered in the cloud of Christ's presence; 4) continual prayer which filled up the cloud for the one and one-half years before revival began; and 5) continuing commitment to praying up a storm.

They asked the Lord for rain in the time of the latter rain, and they received it. This is only the beginning of the outpouring to come. What if churches followed Brownsville's example and disbanded Sunday night services to seek the Lord and pray up a storm?

The Prayer Cycle (Part 2)

God is ready to pour out His Spirit on the cities of America. A city-wide prayer effort will usher in an even far greater manifestation than the one that was experienced in Pensacola. First, we must deal with individual and corporate sin.

Chapter 5

Sins That Hinder

Lamentations 3:44 speaks of God's reaction to Israel's rebellion: "You have covered Yourself with a cloud so that no prayer can pass through" (NAS). Rather than a cloud that should surround us with God's presence, another is used to keep our prayers from His presence. The Bible states that God will not hear the prayers of a person or people of iniquity (see Is. 59:2). Also, First Kings 8:35-36 states:

> *When heaven is shut up, and there is no rain, because they have sinned against Thee; if they pray toward this place* [the place of God's dwelling presence], *and confess Thy name, and turn from their sin, when Thou afflictest them: then hear Thou in heaven, and forgive the sin of Thy servants, and of Thy people Israel, that Thou teach them the good way wherein they should walk, and give rain upon Thy land, which Thou hast given to Thy people for an inheritance.*

Though this was written specifically for Israel, in principle it is applicable for us today. In these verses we find the problem and solutions to the rain's hindrance; the problem, obviously, being that of sin. The solutions were prayer, repentance, and confessing the name of God, which implies making a commitment to live for God. Keep this solution in mind as we look at the hindrances to the latter rain.

The prophet Amos speaks about God's resistance to a proud, idolatrous Israel.

> *And also I have withholden the rain from you, when there were yet three months to the harvest: and I caused it to rain upon one city, and caused it not to rain upon another city: one piece was rained upon, and the piece whereupon it rained not withered. So two or three cities wandered unto one city, to drink water; but they were not satisfied: yet have ye not returned unto Me, saith the Lord* (Amos 4:7-8).

Israel's idolatry and sin brought this judgment by the Lord. Only three months from the harvest and the Lord withheld the latter rain, which would have brought a successful harvest. However, God did more than withhold the rain; He caused it to rain on another city, hoping to provoke Israel to seek Him. People from other cities wandered to the city that received the rain and had water. They drank, yet "were not satisfied."

Another man's revelation, blessing, or gifting will never satisfy us. We often go to seminars and hear how Pastor So-and-So and First Church achieved its growth. Learning from others and gaining fresh insights are good; however, God desires to rain on us, our church, city, and nation just as He did then. The revivals that have broken out in Russia, Korea, China, Africa, and Argentina should cause the Church in America to cry out for its own rain. Pray we do not become so dull as Israel. God rebuked them by saying: "Yet have ye not returned unto Me." God is saying, "After tasting of the blessings I bestowed upon others, I thought you would return to Me and get your own blessing."

ANOTHER MAN'S REVELATION, BLESSING, OR GIFTING WILL NEVER SATISFY US.

Like Israel, America and its church members are in idolatry. Colossians 3:5 states, "…covetousness, which is idolatry." A secular author commented that the one word that describes Americans is "more." The desire for more materially has choked out our spiritual vitality, as Jesus said it would. Just like the present-day American church, Israel had become self-reliant. It had vain confidence in its religious traditions, buildings, and ceremonies. They were no longer a people after God's heart. For this reason,

> THE DESIRE FOR MORE MATERIALLY HAS CHOKED OUT OUR SPIRITUAL VITALITY, AS JESUS SAID IT WOULD.

Amos called Israel to repentance in chapter 5, exhorting them to "Seek the Lord, and ye shall live." We must do the same, or God will resist us by holding back the latter rain.

MORE HINDRANCES

Ye have not, because ye ask not. Ye ask, and receive not, because ye ask amiss, that ye may consume it upon your lusts (James 4:2b-3).

We find two hindrances in these verses. The first hindrance is caused by a lack of prayer due to a lack of faith. We have not the latter rain because we have failed to fervently ask for it. We must ask the Lord for rain in the time of the latter rain.

The second hindrance is caused not because we do not ask, but comes about because of what we ask for. Selfish prayers are a hindrance. They are prayers of manipulation that seek to cut a deal with God if He will only bless us (e.g., "I promise to tithe, God, if You'll get me that job"). God knows our promises are usually short-lived and come from a selfish heart. Of course, we do this in ministry as well, where we seek out God to build our own kingdoms and receive the applause of men. Prayers that will bring the latter rain will be persistent, selfless prayers of faith for God's Kingdom to come and be manifest in every person's life.

Notice that the apostle James ties together a lack of diligence in prayer and lustful prayers. We have heard the saying, "Love can wait, but lust can't." This is true not only for young lovers but for praying saints. If we quickly faint in prayer, perhaps it's because we have lustful prayers. However, prayers that are out of a heart of love for the King will persevere. As the Bible says, "faith…worketh by love" (Gal. 5:6). Prayers of faith that are motivated by a love for Christ and His Kingdom will prevail. Prayers of faith will work because of love, but those motivated by lust will fail.

REPENTANCE REMOVES THE BARRIERS

As we turn from sin, God will turn back the hindering clouds and allow His storm clouds to burst forth with rain. Not only does repentance remove the barriers, but it also prepares us to receive the latter rain.

God showers the earth with rain. However, not all receive the rain in the same proportion. *Water gravitates to its lowest point. Those who will receive the latter rain are those humble, meek seekers who are thirsty for God.*

> *Sow to yourselves in righteousness, reap in mercy; break up your fallow ground* [hardened hearts]: *for it is time to seek the Lord, till He come and rain righteousness upon you* (Hosea 10:12).

> *For thus saith the high and lofty One that inhabiteth eternity, whose name is Holy; I dwell in the high and holy place, with him also that is of a contrite and humble spirit, to revive the spirit of the humble, and to revive the heart of the contrite ones* (Isaiah 57:15).

The high and holy place where God dwells is in the heart of the humble. His manifested presence, through the latter rain, will be perceived by these because He gives grace to the humble (see Jas. 4:6).

Those having the quality of meekness will be reservoirs of the latter rain. James 1:21 says, "Receive with meekness the engrafted word, which is able to save your souls."

Meekness allows God to direct and mold our lives. He may direct us and speak to us in ways that are unconventional to us and which pull us out of our comfort zones. God will rain down His Word in a fresh way. Therefore, we must be meek, which helps us to set aside our preconceived ideas and allows God to direct us.

REPENTANCE BRINGS THE FRUIT

As we humble ourselves and repent, the Word of the Lord is planted in our hearts and is watered by the Holy Spirit. This leads to a life that bears fruit of Christ-like character and ministry.

In Revelation 9:1-5, satan is allowed to unlock the bottomless pit, releasing locusts upon the earth. These locusts are obviously demons. We know that because they are commanded not to hurt "the grass of the earth, neither any green thing, neither any tree; but only those men which have not the seal of God in their foreheads" (v. 4).

The grass of the earth, green things, and trees refer to fruitful men, believers who have been sealed by the Holy Spirit and therefore bear His fruit. Others who are not sealed will be tormented by these demons.

The question I asked myself was, "How does one get the seal of God in one's forehead?" The answer is found in Ezekiel 9:1-4. God told Ezekiel to take an ink kit and "Go through the midst of the city, through the midst of Jerusalem, and set a mark upon the foreheads of the men that sigh and that cry for all the abominations that be done in the midst thereof" (Ezek. 9:4). Those who get the seal of God are those who repent. Those who repent get the Holy Spirit, which causes them to be fruitful. As Isaiah 61:3 stated, "Them that mourn in Zion...might be called trees of righteousness, the planting of the Lord, that He might be glorified."

Those who are repentant, broken, humble, meek seekers will receive the latter rain, which is the manifest presence of God to bring forth "precious fruit."

Of course, bearing the fruits of the Spirit will make us harvesters for His plentiful harvest. As His life is produced in us, we become invincible against the enemy's schemes, for Christ in us is our protection, deliverance, and victory.

EFFECTS OF UNREPENTED SIN

What happens when sin goes unrepented? At the beginning of this chapter I referred to this scripture "You have covered Yourself with a cloud so that no prayer can pass through" (Lam. 3:44 NAS). If the cloud here is a satanic one of darkness, it means God has allowed Apollyon to place it there because of our sin. Our repentance as individuals and a citywide Church is required. This removes the satanic cloud and allows us to place Christ in the heavenly places.

Satanic clouds block our prayers and hide the presence of Christ, without which we cannot be transformed into His image. Yet satan will not only block the blessing of God's presence, and answered prayer, but he will also cause us to be destroyed through this demonic cloud. This destruction is presently being experienced through communities large and small throughout America.

The effects of what is known as "acid rain" symbolize the destructive rain from satan's presence. Water contaminated from oxides of nitrogen and sulfur can combine with water vapor in clouds to form nitric acid. It then falls as acid rain. This rain further pollutes our waters. It also saps the nutrients from the soil and vegetation, which can ultimately destroy plant life.

Our lives of unrepented sin can only produce polluted worship and prayer. It allows the clouds of demonic presence to hover over our lives. As we continue in sin these clouds fill until satan's destructive presence is fully manifested as he rains down evil.

> OUR LIVES OF UNREPENTED SIN CAN ONLY PRODUCE POLLUTED WORSHIP AND PRAYER.

This coincides with the words of Francis Frangipane: "But when the church is passive, indifferent or carnal, the powers of hell increase their rule over the affairs of men; marriages break-up, crime increases and wantonness becomes unbridled."[8]

An example of how a polluted, unrepentant heart produces polluted prayers is found in Allison Mare's book, *The Weapons of Our Warfare.* She asks,

If Satan has been expelled from heaven, how can he continue accusing believers before God? The truth is we often do it for him. While Satan may be barred from heaven, we are invited to enter the most holy place by the blood of Jesus, and to draw near to God (Hebrews 10:19, 22). When we come before the Lord, how will we pray? Will we be intercessors or accusers? What about prayers like, "Dear Lord, please help Mary not to be so angry"? Are not such prayers merely thinly cloaked accusations? If we are to avoid representing Satan before the throne of God, we must make sure our prayer is free from accusation.[9]

Let me add that if we are to avoid praying up and filling a cloud of satanic presence, we must make sure our hearts are free from accusation. If our hearts are free, then our prayers will be as well.

Ms. Mare goes on to comment how we use prayer as a means of gossip and slander. These types of prayers germinate from a heart that is polluted with jealousy, envy, strife, unbelief, etc. Not only is the accuser going before the throne through our prayers, but we are placing him, not Christ, in the heavenly places. As we do so, the devil rains down his destructive purposes over people and cities. As Allison states, "Gossiping for prayer is still gossip and it plays in to the hands of the enemy. What makes us think we can pray effectively when our prayers are based on broken confidence and a form of accusation?"[10]

Christ's presence in the Church is the solution to our cities because a Church filled with Christ can pray in the cloud of His presence and the latter rain upon our communities. As the Church is cleansed by repentance, then Christ will be manifested in the Church and we become healers of our Lord.

CHAPTER 6

Prayers That Overcome Hindering Sin

BREAKTHROUGH PRAYERS

Sins that hinder the rain can be overcome. One Old Testament example tells how sin prevented rain falling from Heaven and even cost lives. However, the prayers of a mother eventually brought the breakthrough. Do you want your prayers answered, especially in regard to seeing your loved ones saved or delivered? The prayers of Rizpah found in Second Samuel 21 bring instruction and encouragement. Let me share the background of this story.

There had been a famine in the land for three years and David asked God as to the reason why. God revealed that the reason was because Saul had killed the Gibeonites. Now to understand what has happened here, you have to go back to Joshua 9 where the Israelites had been defeating all their enemies. The Gibeonites had heard about the Israelite victories and were scared that they would become the next victims. So they came up with a scheme. They dressed themselves in worn-out clothes and sandals and went to see Joshua. Meeting with him, they claimed that they were from a far country and wanted to make covenant with the Israelites. Thus, a peace treaty was established.

Praying Up a STORM

Years later, King Saul decided to kill them, and in doing so, had broken a peace treaty. Although the Gibeonites were a heathen nation, Saul's act still displeased God.

After David had become king, he went to the Gibeonites and asked how he could make it right so that Israel could be delivered from the famine. The Gibeonites rejected the offer of silver and gold—instead they wanted revenge. They wanted someone to pay for Saul's sins; particularly, they wanted the lives of Saul's sons. So David took two sons of Rizpah (concubine of Saul) and five sons of Michal (daughter of Saul). And they were hung on trees on the side of a mountain.

A spiritual parallel can be made here, likening the Gibeonites to the devil, who also cannot be bought. When we sin, he wants us to pay for our sins. He sees it as his assignment to make sure we do. On the other hand, it is God's desire to extend His mercy in spite of our sin, which brings us to Rizpah.

Who was Rizpah? She was the daughter of Aiah and concubine of Saul. She had borne him two sons. I want to center on what Rizpah did in verse 10 of Second Samuel 21 NAS.

> *And Rizpah the daughter of Aiah took sackcloth and spread it for herself on the rock, from the beginning of harvest until it rained on them from the sky; and she allowed neither the birds of the sky to rest on them by day nor the beasts of the field by night.*

While satan, like the Gibeonites, seeks to exact as much punishment as possible, God is looking for someone to give Him a reason to rain down His blessings and mercy. Rizpah was such a woman. Though Rizpah had no hope of seeing her dead sons come back to life, she did pray for God to remove this curse. (Anyone who is hung on a tree is accursed—see Galatians 3:13.) Being hung on a tree symbolized you were

GOD IS LOOKING FOR SOMEONE TO GIVE HIM A REASON TO RAIN DOWN HIS BLESSINGS AND MERCY.

doomed eternally. You would go to sheol and never have hope of Heaven. Therefore, prayer to remove them off the tree and give them a proper burial was to restore their honor and give hope for eternal life with God. Rizpah is a picture of prayer for our children and loved ones who are spiritually dead.

Look at what she did to restore her sons' honor and give hope of life forever: "And Rizpah the daughter of Aiah took sackcloth and spread it for herself on the rock…" (2 Sam. 21:10 NAS).

SHE HAD A GODLY SORROW

Taking sackcloth was an act of mourning. She grieved over the death of her sons. Grieving or mourning is an appropriate action for us to engage in, for our children who are separated from God and are spiritually dead. The act in and of itself is communing with God. One beatitude says, "Blessed are those who mourn for they shall be comforted." Our children's spiritual death must move us to grieve over them. God's heart is broken; and if we are in tune with His heart, our hearts will be broken as well. It is this agreement with God's heart that moves the Father. It was His Son who died so that these would not. It is in grieving that we share in God's heartache for what it took to save His creation. In the grieving, we are comforted with the knowledge that we are sharing in the pain that God feels for a wayward world for whom He sacrificed His only Son.

In addition, her sackcloth was placed upon the *rock*. Second Samuel 22:2 (NAS) states, "The Lord is my rock and my fortress and my deliverer; my God, my rock, in whom I take refuge, my shield and the horn of my salvation." (See also Deuteronomy 32:15.)

We can only speculate concerning Rizpah, but it is possible she knew this scripture. She came to pour her heart out in grief to the Lord as her rock and salvation. Perhaps she repented for any of her own sins and calamity. This kind of situation usually brings this kind of introspection. She perhaps examined her life with King Saul. The Old Testament mind-set was that if such tragedy occurred, it meant someone had sinned. King Saul had sinned and now her sons were paying the price, and she may have been pondering her life and her sons' lives. I choose to believe that Rizpah did not have remorse but true repentance for her own sin and the sin of her sons. It was not a time to shake her fist at God but to truly mourn for their deaths and the sins that had brought them about.

A true mourner is sensitive to his own sins and the sins of others. The Scriptures do not specify but they imply that she not only defended, mourned, and prayed for her own sons but for the sons of Michal as well. It pains mourners to see people cascading in a downward free fall towards hell through carelessly living in sin.

In *The God Chasers,* Tommy Tenney relates a story told to him by a missionary to Argentina in the 1950's—Edward Miller. In the Argentine Bible Institute, 50 students began to pray with a heavy burden for the nation of Argentina. Tenney says, "Dr. Miller told me that those students wept and cried day after day. He mentioned that one young man leaned his head against a concrete brick wall and wept until, after four hours, a trail of tears had run down the porous wall. After six hours had passed, he was standing in a puddle of his own tears! These young intercessors wept day after day, and he said it could only be described as unearthly weeping. These students weren't simply repenting for something they had done. They had been moved by the Spirit into something called 'vicarious repentance,' in which they began to repent for what had happened through others in their city, their region, and in the country of Argentina.[11] Eighteen months later soccer stadiums' capacity seating of 180,000 people were overflowing with evangelists and healing services. The revival was attributed by many to the prayer of repentance wrought by God through 50 students for the nation.

A true mourner will grieve over the sins of others on their behalf when those people do not have the grace to do so themselves. Second Corinthians 7:10 (NAS) says, "For the sorrow that is according to the will of God produces a repentance without regret, leading to salvation, but the sorrow of the world produces death." A godly sorrow that produces repentance which leads to salvation is a *sorrow towards God.*

Rizpah took sackcloth and laid it upon the rock. We do the same when we take the sorrow and sin that has brought spiritual death to our loved ones and place it on the Rock of our salvation, Jesus Christ. We say, "God, I'm sorry for my sins, my children's sins, my spouse's sins. I grieve over the fact You had to die for us. I come humbly acknowledging our sins are against You. Yet, now my loved ones are under the curse of sin for which You died. Please resurrect my children, friends, and loved ones to life eternal."

The beatitude, if you remember, contains a promise. It says, "Blessed are they that mourn for they shall be comforted." Rizpah was comforted with her sons being removed and given a proper burial. As we mourn over the sin of our loved ones, God comforts us in our prayers of intercession. By God's grace, as you pray as Rizpah did, you will know the promise of being comforted by the Holy Spirit who brings salvation to those for whom you are praying.

SHE WARRED IN PRAYER

"And she allowed neither the birds of the sky to rest on them by day nor the beasts of the field by night." The decaying flesh was attracting vultures, jackals, and probably other more formidable animals like lions. Some of these animals were nocturnal in that they only came out at night. Doesn't that sound like our enemy, satan? He loves the darkness and hates the light. Rizpah was swatting birds away night and day. She would hear wild beasts and with all boldness chase them away. Talk about a war cry. Can you envision her screaming at these opportunistic varmints?

Bill Gothard in his book *The Power of Crying Out,* tells a story of a runaway daughter who was influenced by a young man. A mother's war cry caused not only the daughter, but also the young instigator to turn around.

In Melbourne, Australia, this mother was shocked and grieved when her 16-year-old daughter ran off with an older boy. The mother felt this boy had stolen her daughter's affections—that he had somehow convinced her to reject her family and be with him.

The mother had been trying to protect her daughter from wrong friendships and damaging decisions, and now she felt heartsick. Why had God let this happen? There seemed to be no one to whom the mother could turn for help, so she went into a room alone, put a towel over her mouth to muffle the sound of her cry, and with all her strength cried out, "O God, deliver my daughter from this boy!"

The next day the mother and father learned about one of Mr. Gothard's ministry seminars in Melbourne. They decided to go and also to invite their daughter to attend. To their amazement, she agreed.

The daughter liked the session so much that she asked her boyfriend to go with her the next night. He came, and became so convicted that he repented of what he'd done in taking the girl away and asked both the Lord and the girl's parents to forgive him. The two young people agreed to separate from each other so that each one could grow in faith in the Lord and rebuild family relationships.[12]

We are fighting for those who cannot fight for themselves. Their lives are worth the battle. Rizpah was resigned to this task. She was ready to fight night and day if need be for her sons' honor. Their eternal rest was more important than her being inconvenienced, facing danger, and suffering. She probably endured some battle scars inflicted by these birds and beasts, but she was not about to give up her post.

An article by John Piper called, "Prayer: The Power That Wields The Weapon," shares our need to recognize the war we are in and to wield prayer as our greatest weapon.

The problem is that most Christians don't really believe that life is war and that our invisible enemy is awesome. How then, can we ever convince them to pray? They say they believe these truths, but their daily lives reveal otherwise. There is a peacetime casualness in the church about spiritual things. There are no bombs falling in their circumstances, no bullets whizzing overhead, no mines to avoid, no roars on the horizon; all is well in America, the Disneyland of the universe. So why pray?

In wartime, newspaper headline stories report what the troops are facing and how they are faring. During wartime, families get together, talk about their sons and daughters on the frontlines, and pray with wrenching concern for their safety. In wartime people are alert, armed, and vigilant. People spend their money so differently during conflict than in peacetime. There's an austerity and simplicity of life, not because such things are so valuable in themselves, but because there's something grand about a cause greater than wallpapering your den. Everybody is touched in wartime; everyone cuts back.

> THE PROBLEM IS THAT MOST CHRISTIANS DON'T REALLY BELIEVE THAT LIFE IS WAR AND THAT OUR INVISIBLE ENEMY IS AWESOME.

If we're going to mobilize a movement of prayer in our churches and cities, if we're going to sustain a heart for prayer, we must truly believe that life is war. We must get out of the peacetime mentality. Until we feel the desperation of a bombing raid and the thrill of a new offensive against the forces of darkness, we will not pray the way we should.[13]

SHE PERSEVERED IN PRAYER

Rizpah is a picture of persevering prayer. How long was she out there? It says, "...from the first day of harvest until it rained on them from the sky" (v. 10 NAS). The first day of harvest on the Jewish calendar is March 15, and the rain usually came around October 15. For seven long months, Rizpah prayed, defended the decaying bodies, yelled, cried night and day, and exposed herself to the elements. Imagine how she might have looked with her skin baked by the sun, her lips cracked and bleeding from the dry wind, and her clothes in disarray. Rizpah had a resolve to see her task through, no matter what it took.

Praying Up a STORM

During this time as she continued to lament and cry out to God, the bodies were decaying. Satan, the liar, was then able to use the stench from her sons' bodies to tell her that there was no hope, it was a lost cause, and she should just give up. As you labor in prayer, perhaps you see those for whom you are praying decaying further spiritually. The devil speaks unbelief and doubt to your heart in hopes that you will quit altogether. Do not lose heart. God hears the cry of the desperate and will attend unto your prayer.

Seemingly as each day passed, her prayers went unanswered. Like Israel, who was experiencing the worst possible drought in the natural, spiritually Rizpah's family members were dead, dishonored, and cursed; and Heaven was silent. But the Rock she was perpetually leaning on became a symbol of hope. It is possible that without it she would have given up. The rock reminded her that, "The Lord is my Rock…my deliverer…and the horn of my salvation" (2 Sam. 22:2). The New Testament tells us we have a more sure hope. Hebrews 7:19 tells us we have a better hope in Christ. We have the possibility of seeing our loved ones and children being resurrected through Jesus Christ in this life and the next.

For those who cry out day and night Jesus says, "I tell you that He [God] will bring about justice for them quickly"(Luke 18:8 NAS). King David finally heard what she had done and how she had sacrificed. He ordered that their bodies be taken down along with the bones of Saul and Jonathan and he gave them an honorable burial. King David is a type of King Jesus. As the heart of David was moved by the mourning, warring, and persevering prayers of Rizpah, how much more is our Lord Jesus moved. I believe such prayers quickly ascend and our God speedily responds. Be confident your prayers are not in vain and will bring honor and salvation to those you love.

I am reminded of a story by Jane Hansen that she tells about her son, Jeff. Jeff's life started to spiral downward in junior high school when he became involved with the wrong crowd. He eventually left home, and his life's conditions continued to worsen. She writes,

Prayers That Overcome Hindering Sin

> I can't tell you the incredible pain I experienced during that period of my life. I was a Christian; I cried out to God, yet all I had hoped and believed for my son's life was slipping out of reach. I tried to talk with my husband, but it was a difficult time in our marriage. We weren't able to connect in a way that would have given me the strength and support I needed...I was sick with worry and heartbroken with grief over what was occurring in my family. Chaos and tension permeated our home, affecting our two younger children as well.

As Jane was ironing one day, the Lord spoke to her and said, "It is My desire to restore—not primarily for your sake, but for Mine. You will reap the overflow." Jane started to press into God for answers through the Word and prayer. She studied Proverbs 31 and discovered what it really means to be a virtuous woman—a strong and able person. The virtuous woman is one of might and power, a woman who is "war worthy." Someone who is war worthy is ready to go to war and has one thought in mind—to win. Jane realized that she was involved in a war for her son's life and she had a resolve in her heart to do everything in her power to win!

It is interesting to note that the Hebrew word for *virtuous* also means "to labor, to travail and bring forth life." Most of us know how to bring forth life in the natural. And just as God has created us to bring life in the physical, so has He also placed a capacity in us to travail and bring to birth things in the spiritual realm.

Thus, Jane started to feel like a woman "great with child." The spirit of intercession started to consume her. She further writes,

> At the time, I knew little about intercession. What I did know was that this child of mine was headed for destruction and the weight and grief of the situation led me to cry out to God. There were days when I would prostrate myself on the floor, my only prayers being unintelligible groans and travail,

weeping before God. At other times, as I was going about my daily routine, I would sense a heaviness, a knowing that I needed to pray.[14]

Jane became bold in her prayers saying, "Lord, I release him to You. I don't just want a young man who is cleaned up and off drugs—do whatever You have to do to bring forth a man of God."

Jane continued to speak aloud the promises of God from His Word over her son's life. She did it as she prayed, while working around the house, driving the car—continually inviting the Holy Spirit to have full control. About six months later, Jeff experienced a complete turnaround in his life. God is also concerned about your children and loved ones. "They may be old enough to run faster than you can, but they can't run faster than God."[15]

Jesus, who lives to make intercession, was appropriating Rizpah's prayers and tears so that the Father would rain down His mercy on the land.

Pray the following so that your loved ones will never see spiritual death but continually know life under the protective cloud of God's presence and favor.

Pray the cloud of Christ's presence over your children or loved ones so that they:

- Will know Christ as Savior early in life (Psalm 63:1; 2 Timothy 3:15).

- Will have a hatred for sin (Psalm 97:10).

- Will be caught when guilty (Psalm 119:71).

- Will be protected from the evil one in each area of their lives: spiritual, emotional, and physical (John 17:15).

- Will have a responsible attitude in all their interpersonal relationships (Daniel 6:3).

- Will respect those in authority over them (Romans 13:1).

- Will desire the right kind of friends and be protected from the wrong friends (Proverbs 1:10-11).

- Will be kept from the wrong mate and saved for the right one (2 Corinthians 6:14-17).

- As well as those they marry, will be kept pure until marriage (1 Corinthians 6:18,20).

- Will learn to totally submit to God and actively resist satan in all circumstances (James 4:7).

- Will be single-hearted and sold out to Jesus Christ (Romans 12:1-2).

- Will be hedged in so they cannot find their way to wrong people or wrong places and that the wrong people cannot find their way to them (Hosea 2:6).

- Will grow and deepen their relationship in Jesus Christ through God's Word and prayer (1 Peter 2:2).

- Will be sensitive to the work of the Holy Spirit in their lives (Galatians 5:25)

I want you to understand that Rizpah was warring over bodies that would never come to life again. She was basically warring for their honor. But unlike Rizpah, we have the hope of seeing our loved ones come back to life. Our children, husbands, or loved ones may be experiencing spiritual death as a result of their sin, and you may see no sign of repentance on their part. So as a child of the King, you need to repent and mourn on their behalf. We repent on the Rock for their spiritual death and cry out for their rebirth. The King is hearing our cries and is responding to our intercessions.

Are you willing to go through the drought time? Are you ready and determined to see the task through? It may take months or years to see the fruits of your prayers. Have you counted the cost of what it will take to bring your loved ones or friends to salvation?

Praying Up a STORM

Just as Jesus is the *Rock* of our salvation, He can be the *Rock* for our loved ones and friends as well. He is there to help us when we feel like giving up because they keep rejecting the gospel, or when we become frustrated with their lifestyle (the smell of sin), or when we are simply just tired of trying and see no results.

Come to the *Rock* and spread your sackcloth—that pain, despair, hurt, fears, rejection, and frustration. You can make a difference in the outcome of your loved ones' spiritual lives. You can bring the honor of salvation to their lives through your prayers. Come to the *Rock!*

CHAPTER 7

Christ's Presence Over Your City

DISPLACING THE DARKNESS

From the following verses, we will see that the cloud of Christ's presence is the key to the harvest. The presence of Christ causes people to repent and cast off idols. It will melt hearts of stone, causing them to recognize Jesus Christ as Lord. Isaiah 19:1 says the Lord "rideth upon a swift cloud, and shall come into Egypt: and the idols of Egypt shall be moved at His presence, and the heart of Egypt shall melt in the midst of it."

If the presence of Christ will bring the harvest, we must pray in the cloud of God's glorious presence.

> *And I looked, and behold a white cloud, and upon the cloud one sat like unto the Son of man, having on His head a golden crown, and in His hand a sharp sickle. And another angel came out of the temple, crying with a loud voice to Him that sat on the cloud, Thrust in Thy sickle, and reap: for the time is come for Thee to reap; for the harvest of the earth is ripe. And He that sat on*

the cloud thrust in His sickle on the earth; and the earth was reaped (Revelation 14:14-16).

This passage gives us a picture of the reality in the heavenly realm before the great end-time harvest. In these verses, Christ is seated on a white cloud with a sharp sickle in His hand. An angel enters announcing the harvest is ripe. From this cloud, He thrusts His sickle and reaps the great end-time harvest from the earth. Christ seated on the white cloud represents His being seated in the heavenly realms. It speaks of His presence enveloping the earth. The cloud of His presence prayed up over the earth makes the harvest ripe and ready to be reaped. I believe we, the Church, could be that sharp sickle in His hand. The biblical word "sharp" represents a people in spiritual shape and ready to give an answer for the hope we have in Christ Jesus, thus reaping the harvest.

C. Peter Wagner and Francis Frangipane are two authors who give insight into spiritual warfare in the heavenly realms. I will demonstrate how the cloud of Christ's presence agrees with their teachings and, indeed, is a key to the harvest. C. Peter Wagner cites three levels of spiritual warfare: the ground level, the occult level, and the strategic level. Each level demonstrates a hierarchy of demonic activity. The ground level is casting out devils (see Acts 19:11-12), the occult level is religious strongholds (see Acts 19:19), and the strategic level is principalities and powers in the heavenly realms (see Eph. 6:12).

It is interesting that there are three major levels of cloud formation which parallel Wagner's levels: the stratocumulus, or nimbostratus, 7000 feet and below; the cirrostratus, from 7000 to 20,000 feet; and the cirrocumulus, or altostratus, 20,000 feet and above. There is a fourth cloud, which covers each of the areas. It is the cumulonimbus. It can range up to eight miles high from top to bottom and brings heavy downpours of rain.

CHRIST'S PRESENCE OVER YOUR CITY

	C. Peter Wagner	Francis Frangipane *Three Battlegrounds*	The Way to Victory	Main Levels of Cloud Formation
1	Ground Level- casting out devils Acts 19:11-12	The Mind	The individual having fellowship with Christ in the heavenly places. Eph. 2:6	Stratocumulus and Nimbostratus 7,000 feet and below
2	Occult Level- religious strongholds Acts 19:19	The Church	The Church operating in the heavenly realms through Christ. Eph. 3:10-12	Cirrostratus 7,000-20,000
3	Strategic Level- principalities and powers in the heavenly realms Eph. 6:12	The Heavenly Realms	Christ in heavenly places. Eph. 1:21-22	Cirrocumulus or Altostratus 20,000 feet and above
4			Final victory when all things are summed up in Christ. Eph. 1:10	Cumulonimbus - tall cumulus clouds that bring thick, heavy downpours of rain—up to 8 miles high.**

**Praying in the cloud of God's presence covers every spiritual realm pouring down the latter rain.

Another similarity is found in Francis Frangipane's book *The Three Battlegrounds*. Frangipane states that the three areas of warfare are the mind, the Church, and the heavenly places. Again, we have three levels. The key to victory is the Church placing Christ in the heavenly places. As Frangipane states:

> All spiritual warfare is waged over one essential question. Who will control reality on earth; Heaven or Hell? When it comes to angelic and demonic warfare, the battle rests not in physical weaponry, but in the power of agreement between mankind and the spirit realm. We read in Ephesians 6 that "...principalities and power" occupy the "heavenly places" (verse 12). But we read in Ephesians 1:10 that it is the Father's expressed purpose to sum up all things in Christ, "...things in the heavens and things upon the earth." Ephesians 3:10 reveals God's glorious plan, that through the church God has purposed to make known His manifold wisdom "...unto the principalities and powers in the heavenly places!" You

see, as the body of Christ on earth agrees with its Head in Heaven, the Spirit of Christ Himself displaces the powers of darkness in the heavenly places.

In other words, when the church on earth is aggressive in its agreement with the will and Work of God, then the Presence of God increases in the spiritual realm, proportionally displacing the influence of hell on earth. Shortly thereafter, manifesting in the world of men, we see revivals, healings and miracles. But when the church is passive, indifferent or carnal, the powers of hell increase their rule over the affairs of men: marriages break up, crime increases and wantonness become unbridled. We must see that our prayers, attitudes and agreement with God are an integral part of establishing the reality of the Kingdom of God on earth![16]

The cloud of God's presence dispels the presence of the enemy (see Eph.1:20-21). As Christ then rains down on our churches, communities, and nations, a harvest of souls will be wrought.

Remember, clouds represent the presence of Christ. The key to victory is to place the cloud of Christ's presence at every level. Then, He can and will rain down His manifest blessings. This is what the Ephesian church experienced. They were "blessed...with all spiritual blessings in heavenly places in Christ" (Eph. 1:3). The Ephesians experienced the former rain. God rained down His Word and supernatural giftings of the Holy Spirit (see Acts 19:11-12). Harvesters were raised up harvesting souls throughout Asia Minor. "All they which dwelt in Asia heard the word of the Lord Jesus, both Jews and Greeks" (Acts 19:10). This is evidenced by the churches planted through the church of Ephesus (the seven churches of Revelation 2 and 3).

> THE KEY TO VICTORY IS TO PLACE THE CLOUD OF CHRIST'S PRESENCE AT EVERY LEVEL.

Christ's Presence Over Your City

The Spirit's activity in Ephesus may be considered ground and occult level activity (souls being saved, devils being cast out). C. Peter Wagner, in his "Advancing the Kingdom Prayer Seminar," stated, "Paul did not confront the goddess Diana because it was not God's timing in the spiritual realm." However, tradition has it that years later John did confront the idol of Diana in her temple and in moments it crumbled. Since the idol of Diana crumbled immediately for John, why did Paul avoid the same confrontation?

The timing for such confrontation was not right for Paul, and he knew it. What made the timing right was the prayers of the church at Ephesus. They obeyed Paul's instruction concerning placing Christ in the heavenly places and fighting the spiritual warfare (see Eph. 6:12). They prayed in the cloud of Christ's presence in each level. Winning the war in the heavenly realms made the confronting of the demons behind the idol of Diana a mere formality. The confrontation was a blowout resulting in the shattering of the idol and its power.

In the beginning satan was banished from the presence of God forever. Therefore, to pray up the cloud of Christ's presence means that satan cannot enter that region even if he wanted to. That being the case, to pray up the cloud of Christ's presence dispels satan's influence.

However, this placing Christ in the heavenlies, which Frangipane calls the principal of displacement (the ushering in of Christ's presence which flushes out satan), is not an individual or local church effort, but a corporate Church effort in each community. Placing the cloud of Christ's presence so He can pour out the Spirit's blessing takes a citywide effort.

In his book *Prayer Evangelism,* Ed Silvoso writes:

> It is possible to remove the devil from our homes, our neighborhoods, our cities and our states. By removing I mean to take away from Satan the upper hand he has enjoyed for so long in the spirit

world, so that the Church has the advantage instead. We have seen this happen in cities, and now we are beginning to see it take place in regions and in nations, as in the case of Singapore, the Philippines and others....It is possible for the Church to take control of the spiritual climate, but it requires a concerted, enveloping movement....[17]

Whether you can agree with C. Peter Wagner, Francis Frangipane, or myself about the three levels of activity in the spiritual realm is not the most important fact here. What is important is that you do understand satan is at work in the spiritual realm and your prayers are used by Christ to dispel satan's influence in lives, cities, and whole regions. Therefore, pray individually and corporately for Christ to move in and satan's influence to leave.

CHRIST, THE HOPE FOR THE CITIES

If the Church does not have the solution to our cities' problems in these last days, then we will have cities with no solutions.

Said positively, the Spirit-filled Church is the only hope for our cities, for the solution is Christ manifested among us. Proverbs 16:15 states, *"In the light of the king's countenance is life; and his favour is as a cloud of the latter rain."* The evidence of having the favor of King Jesus is the cloud of His presence, which brings the latter rain.

The Church can do nothing in and of itself. The solution is Christ manifested in the Church. The Christ-filled Church joined together to bring the manifest presence of Christ to our cities is the ultimate answer. Gaining Christ's favor as seen in the cloud of the latter rain is essential.

Therefore, the first step of the corporate Church in any city is repentance. The sins of the city, even of those of the forefathers of a city, need to be recognized and denounced and forgiveness sought. When I speak of citywide, I am referring to the citywide Church, which is responsible for the moral and spiritual climate in the community.

Before the Israelites could take the city of Jericho, God had called Joshua to have all the men circumcised (see Josh. 5:1-10). Jericho was to be a spiritual battle, not a physical one. The instruments for final victory were to be the blowing of trumpets and shouts of praise. God needed these instruments (people) of war to be totally surrendered to Him. Circumcision was the sign that these men belonged to the Lord. Without circumcision, the Israelites would be ineffective against the spiritual forces over Jericho.

If our prayers and praise are to be effective, we must circumcise our hearts through repentance. Halfhearted lives that are mixed with lives yielded to the flesh and not to the Spirit will bring about polluted prayers and praises that will be ineffectual against the principalities and powers over our cities. Therefore, we must repent and remove all the works of the flesh in our lives. The Church as a whole needs to repent for its complacency and love for amusements and entertainment. The Church must be circumcised unto Christ in order to take the city.

The word *circumcision* literally means, "to make a circle." Remember, part of the plan of God for the Israelites to conquer the city of Jericho was to circle that city for seven days. The Israelites, having circumcised themselves unto God, had the spiritual authority to circle (circumcise) and literally cut off satan's power and influence over Jericho. As the Israelites praised God with the trumpets and their voices, the presence of God came in and dispelled satan's domain over Jericho and the promised land.

The principle learned is that as we are surrendered completely to Christ, the enemy is cut off from us. Therefore, we gain the spiritual authority to cut off the enemy's presence from our lives and his power over our city. We can cut off the enemy's influence or circumcise our communities the same way the Israelites did Jericho. The Israelites walked around or made a circle around Jericho, thus circumcising it spiritually. Through prayer walking in our neighborhoods, we can do the same. As we circumcise our own hearts from sin and set them apart unto the Lord, we gain spiritual authority. This authority is to circumcise or cut off the enemy's influence over our neighbors. As each one covers his or her neighborhood, we, block by block, neighborhood by neighborhood, circumcise our city, state, and nation. Eugene Peterson's rendering of John 1:14 in his paraphrase Bible, *The Message,* says, "And the Word became flesh and blood and moved into the neighborhood."[18] As we who are filled by God's Spirit prayerwalk our neighborhoods and pray for our businesses, God through our flesh and blood once again moves into the neighborhoods and inhabits our communities.

Steve Hawthorne, in his book coauthored with Graham Kendrick entitled *Prayerwalking: Praying On-site With Insight,* has written one of the best books on prayerwalking published by Creation House. Steve provides some good tools to help you begin and pray the Scriptures over your neighbors. Check out his resources at: www.waymakers.org. You can join hundreds of others who are praying for their neighbors and register as a "Lighthouse of Prayer" at www.lighthousemovement.com.

When the people of Nineveh removed the cloud of judgment over themselves by repenting, God visited them with a citywide revival. He can do it again. As we, the Church, repent and circumcise our spiritual hearts, we remove sin and the cloud of judgment over our cities.

HOUSTON'S PRAYER MOUNTAIN

The citywide Church in Houston, Texas recently experienced the benefits of corporate repentance. Doug Stringer, founder of Turning Point Ministries, rallied 200 churches and 150 ministries for 40 days of prayer and fasting at Houston's Prayer Mountain.

CHRIST'S PRESENCE OVER YOUR CITY

Each night the service lasted five to six hours. Great purging, brokenness, and repentance took place in the hearts of pastors and all believers. God grew in the hearts of the believers in Houston.

Claire Green, youth pastor at Glorious Way Church in Houston, reports, "One could come to any Prayer Mountain meeting and expect to see some sort of visible wall being torn down. Denominational barriers melted as worship teams from various backgrounds took the stage each night."

Ethnic and racial barriers crumbled as well. Palestinians embraced Jews, and Jews embraced Germans in public displays of Christian brotherhood. Chinese and Japanese leaders prayed for one another. Anglo, African, and Hispanic Americans alike shared in praise.

David Yuan, worship leader at Grace Community Fellowship and a Chinese American, observed, "Interracially, interdenominationally and interculturally, God is doing a work of unity that breaks through all the personal bondage and all the social problems we have."

At Houston's Prayer Mountain, believers not only battled the social evil of prejudice, but also that of poverty. During the 40 days, Turning Point funneled almost $35,000 in financial aid, most of which was collected at Prayer Mountain, for ministries in need.

And the giving didn't stop with money. Area churches donated loads of clothes, blankets, food, and enough toys to ensure that more than 600 children had presents on Christmas morning.

National ministries also helped out. Operation Blessing's Hunger Strike Force provided enough groceries for 5,000 needy families on December 7. Then on December 14, GOAD International provided more than 40,000 pounds of food and 1,000 blankets for distribution through various "Somebody Cares Houston" outreach ministries and churches.

Praying Up a STORM

Doug Stringer states, "Since Prayer Mountain, the water level of the Holy Spirit has risen in the city. Consequently, many churches are experiencing an increase in salvations, attendance, and a sincere hunger to know Christ in a deeper way among their members."[19]

The corporate Church will, like that of Houston's Prayer Mountain, return to prayer and see the presence of Christ prevail in the heavenly places over our cities. Dr. Terry Teykl reports many churches are returning to prayer:

> Many citywide prayer movements are springing up today. In Los Angeles, 300 to 1,000 pastors gather every quarter to pray for their city and nation. In Cleveland, Ohio, 6,000 to 7,000 people take part in citywide rallies. Three hundred churches in Minneapolis, Minnesota met in the Metrodome and committed to pray for their cities for seven years.[20]

In the city of Osaka, Japan, Paul K. Ariga mobilized 9,000 intercessors providing 180,000 hours of prayer for a three-night crusade that took place in the city's 60,000-seat baseball stadium. Many cities are following the examples I have stated. They are praying in the cloud of God's presence over their city and nation. They are praying in the latter rain to reap the end-time harvest.

If I were to make a prediction for rain in one city, it would be Kansas City. Here is why: Mike Bickle, former pastor of the Kansas City Fellowship, has organized 400 full-time intercessors to pray for their city. These 400 warriors have raised their own support. (He was expecting another 300 to be added before the year 2003 ended.) Intercession and worship is taking place 24 hours a day through these full-time prayer laborers and others.

In Numbers 16:41-50, a plague had spread among the people of Israel because of their grumbling and false accusations against Moses and Aaron. God was so disgusted with their actions that He wanted to destroy all of them, but Moses and Aaron fell on their faces and pleaded with God for the lives of their people.

Moses then told Aaron to take action. "Get the censer from the altar and put fire in it, and incense to burn on the fire. Take the censer and go among the people and stand between the living and the dead." As he did so, the plague was stopped.

In America, we have a nation that is worse than Israel. We have most of the world's goods, but too often we are the worst complainers. It's evident that the plague of sin is rampant.

We stated earlier in this book that we are the current priests, and the incense refers to the prayers of the saints. God is fed up with the arrogance and complaining lips of America. His judgment would be swift and total if not for His people who go and take the incense called prayer and "stand between the living and the dead," not to save America, but to save those infected with the plague of sin, which will bring death.

We are called to go among the people with prayer (incense) and to stand between the living and the dead. Our prayers will be the difference between life and death for many. Go among the people where you work, in your neighborhood, and school—whatever your surroundings might be.

> OUR PRAYERS WILL BE THE DIFFERENCE BETWEEN LIFE AND DEATH FOR MANY.

Joe Brown, who has a prayer ministry in Tampa, Florida relates a story that illustrates the effects of praying wherever you may be:

> One night in February 1997, I went to pick up my wife at the cancer hospital where she was working. When I arrived at the hospital and went to her floor, she told me she needed more time to finish the reports on her patients. So I went down to the main lobby to sit and wait for her. As I was sitting there, I felt an impression from the Lord to pray over the

hospital. I prayed for God to pour out His Spirit and His saving power and bring salvation, blessing, and peace to all those who worked there. I also prayed that He would reveal Himself to the patients in a healing way and to greatly encourage their families.

After praying for a few minutes, I looked up to see a patient, who was a lady dressed in a light blue robe, walking through the lobby. When I saw her, I felt an impression from the Lord to pray for her, although I did not know the lady and had never seen her before. While my head was bowed and I was praying for her and asking God to speak to her heart, she came over to me and touched my shoulder and said, "Are you meditating or resting your eyes?" I responded, "Neither. I was praying…praying for you." Immediately she began weeping. Then she said, "At one time in my life I was walking close to the Lord, but I have drifted far away from Him. My husband abused me and my children were taken away. Now I have cancer and I am very sick. I know I need to get right with God. Would you please pray for me?" By that time my wife was there, so we joined hands with this dear lady, and as I was praying for her she fell to her knees weeping, repenting of her sins, and making her peace with God right in the middle of the lobby of the hospital.[21]

Such instances are possible on a frequent, even daily basis as we make ourselves available to God, with the desire to bring His presence known and felt in the marketplace. Joe Brown is one who is leading through example. More like him are needed to see God rain down revival!

Chapter 8

Leaders Leading the Way to Revival

CORPORATE LEADERSHIP

The phrase "one accord" literally means to have one, united, burning desire or burden. The first Church had that desire, and the Holy Spirit shook the building and the known world for Christ (see Acts 4:24,31).

The Lord Jesus desires to shake our land. He will do so as those who are filled with the Holy Spirit are in one accord, having one burning desire to see Jesus reign as King in our land.

Our chief end as the Church of Jesus Christ is to pray, "Thy kingdom come, Thy will be done." God has so privileged us in His relationship with us. Our relationship has a purpose—praying down God's blessing on others. Pray Kingdom blessings on them, and pray that Christ would rule their lives.

When Jesus sent His disciples into the city, He told them to proclaim, "The kingdom of heaven is at hand" (Mt. 10:7). Do our communities see or detect the Kingdom of God at hand?

No, they see the kingdom of Baptist, Methodist, charismatic, and so forth. However, united around the King Jesus Christ, the community will experience His Kingdom authority. His Kingdom will come in fullness to our area as we begin to understand our tasks as part of the whole. His Kingdom coming in fullness to our area is a task much larger than any one church or ministry can accomplish. We must recognize the entire mission God wants to accomplish and join it.

STEPS TO USHERING IN THE GLORY

In Second Chronicles 5, we again find the Old Testament being a shadow of spiritual realities. Regarding the dedication of the temple, principles for ushering in the manifested presence and glory of God into the city Church are seen.

First, notice in verse 2 that all the leaders were assembled together for this event. The Promise Keepers stadium events are evidence of spiritual power that is present when leadership comes together. It is necessary for church leaders to come together in unity in order to see a move of God in their cities.

HOW CAN WE GET THESE LEADERS TO ASSEMBLE?

There was a common point that brought these leaders in Israel together—the dedication of the temple. God is using citywide prayer to unify the Body today and demonstrate dedication to Him.

At the temple dedication, each of the leaders was going to participate in something bigger than himself. Leaders need to see that there is something God desires to do in their city, which is bigger than their sphere of responsibility and influence. However, at the same time, the leaders of your city need to realize that the big picture God desires to accomplish cannot be done without their cooperation. Pastors often fail to see how participation in the citywide church movements is beneficial to their churches. When God pours out the latter rain on a city, everyone will get their buckets filled.

Secondly, the Levites were to bring the ark of the covenant into the temple. The Israelites understood and knew that their God was a God of covenant. As we acknowledge the covenant Christ has made for us and exercise that covenant by accepting and loving others in the Kingdom of God, we will be blessed. Paul tells us that we are to have one mind, and that we are to do nothing through strife or vain glory (see Phil. 2:2-3).

Walking out covenant relationships through love and forgiveness is the only way we can experience the blessing of God's manifest presence in our cities. Christ died so that we might be a people through whom He would have a witness to the world. As we walk in covenant relationships and put away the spirit of competition, pride, and church "upmanship," we should expect God's blessing (see Ps. 133:3). If God has commanded it, then there is nothing that can stop it.

Thirdly, sacrifices were made. Solomon and all the people sacrificed more sheep and oxen than could be counted (see 2 Chron. 5:6). Were there a bunch of lazy ushers who were not up to counting all the sheep, or were there truly too many to count? How many sheep and oxen were sacrificed? In Second Chronicles 7:5, after the glory of the Lord fell in the temple, they sacrificed one hundred and twenty thousand sheep and twenty-two thousand oxen. The number of sacrifices would seem to be well beyond what could be counted. The bottom line is that there was blood everywhere. King Solomon, down to the average Israelite, was covered with blood from the slaughter. Blood was flowing from the temple.

No matter who you are, you must be covered with the blood. Some of us feel unworthy to approach God for His outpouring of His presence or for a move of God. I guarantee you these Israelites were not perfect, but they were covered by the blood. When God looked down, He did not see their sins and faults. He saw only blood. Similarly, God's people are not worthy of a move of God. But

God does not see our faults; He sees only the blood of His Son, which covers us all.

It has been said that all ground is level at the cross. Solomon was no better than anyone else. He also was involved in the sacrifice. God has given men gifts and responsibilities in the Kingdom, but that defines function only, not status. With an attitude that sees ourselves as equal under the blood, we can boldly approach God for our need of an outpouring of His Spirit.

Paul's desire for the Philippian church was that they would be "likeminded, having the same love, being of one accord, of one mind" (Phil. 2:2). Paul was expressing Christ's desire for His Church. Leadership of the local body of Christ must have His desire for oneness and seek to bring it about.

The attitude to achieve such oneness is in the following verse of Philippians 2: "in lowliness of mind let each esteem other better than themselves" (v. 3). God became a man and a servant and was obedient even to the most humiliating of deaths, a death on a cross. Unity will be achieved as leadership develops this mind, which was in Christ Jesus, and is willing to make the sacrifices.

Everyone was unified in bringing sacrifices to the dedication of the temple. This temple was a vehicle through which God was glorified and His presence was made known to all the earth (see 1 Kings 8:60). We all must make sacrifices for unity to be achieved so that God will once again be glorified and His presence manifested through the living temple called His Church.

Most of us need to offer our schedules and become available to what God wants to do. The leadership must sacrifice their titles, positions, and their need for notoriety. We must yield our own kingdoms and even programs to which many of our members are enslaved, and release those people to pursue what God desires to do in their cities. Christ is calling all believers in America, and especially Christian leaders, to offer the sacrifice of fasting for revival.

Leaders Leading the Way to Revival

Sacrifices are made for a greater good. We have to give up what we believe is a good thing for the "God thing" He is doing. Through these sacrifices we speak to God, and by our actions we come into agreement with God. We say, "God, we are decreasing so You might increase. We agree that You desire to bring Heaven down to earth in our city, and we are willing to make these sacrifices so that You will do so." *Remember, we do not make sacrifices to be worthy of revival, but to be ready for it.* God will visit such people.

> REMEMBER, WE DO NOT MAKE SACRIFICES TO BE WORTHY OF REVIVAL, BUT TO BE READY FOR IT.

We find later in Second Chronicles 7 that the Lord came down in glory and fire from Heaven and consumed the sacrifices. In the consuming of the sacrifices, God was saying, "I am pleased." When God visits our cities, He again is saying, "I accept and approve of the sacrifices you have made to see My glory manifested among men."

We have already mentioned praise as a means of filling up the cloud and seeing God's glory descend. Leaders, leading the worship, demonstrate an exaltation of who God is and what He means to us. Again, through worship we say, "Increase, Lord. Let all the world know You are Lord." As they were praising the Lord, the visitation happened. Again, let me add the comment of Solomon: "The Lord has said that He would dwell in the thick cloud" (2 Chron. 6:1 NAS)—the cloud of His presence.

In chapter 6 of Second Chronicles, Solomon ended his prayer by saying, "Now therefore arise, O Lord God, to Your resting place, You, and the ark of Your might: let Your priests, O Lord God, be clothed with salvation and let Your godly ones rejoice in what is good" (v. 41 NAS). Solomon was saying, *"Take Your resting place on the throne of Heaven and sovereignly rule and reign over Israel."* God did just that. Israel enjoyed 40 years of peace through Solomon's reign during which time Israel's wealth, strength, and territory greatly expanded.

I submit to you that what Solomon asked God to do in verse 42 is the same thing Paul reminds us of in Ephesians 1:3. Paul said that Christ was seated, rested and reigning in the heavenly realms. Just as Solomon and the Israelites produced conditions to see the heavenly reality of Christ rule on the earth, so must we. The Ephesian church seemingly obeyed Paul's instruction, and greatly expanded and enjoyed prosperity and victory over their enemies, as did Israel in Solomon's day. This church planted six out of the seven churches in the region of Asia Minor that we read about in Revelation.

The blessing of citywide revival comes as leadership is unified in purpose and walks in covenant relationships. The glory of God will come into our cities as a thick cloud, as we make the necessary sacrifices and worship, and praise and pray together. It's time for every church in the city to become the healthy, prayer-focused church He desires.

VIAGRA CHURCH?

I believe we have too many "Viagra churches"—those churches that portray healthy aspects, but in reality are artificial, and cannot sustain that condition. Viagra for a man's sexual life may be acceptable, but a Viagra church is completely unacceptable. A Viagra church uses programs that attempt to hype life into its otherwise dead or impotent ministries and congregation.

What every church must realize is that, on its own, it has a problem with impotence. How you handle the problem is the key. We can get the next best method, an upcoming band or speaker, or the most promising church growth program, but we will show life and vigor for only a short time. Churches must declare that they are impotent by themselves and demonstrate that they are wholly dependent upon our omnipotent God through prayer. The solution to the viagra Church is the presence based Church. My friend Terry Teykl describes the presence based Church as where members ask after the service "I hope God enjoyed that today?" Whereas, the viagra consumer based Church will ask following worship "I hope the people enjoyed that today?" The difference is the first seeks to please God and the later seeks to please man. Corporately as we seek Him we will encounter the rain of His presence which alone satisfies our greatest need.

"UNION" IS OUR DELIVERER

Judges 3 tells how the sins of the Israelites allowed their enemy, the Moabites, to possess the Promised Land and dominate them for 18 years. The people of Israel desperately cried out to the Lord for a deliverer. The Lord raised up Ehud, who gave the fat King Eglon a message from God. The message came in the form of a double-edged sword plunged into his belly. The Bible reports, "...their lord was fallen down dead on the earth" (Judg. 3:25).

Ehud then went and rallied all the people because the Lord had given their enemy into their hands. They routed the Moabites, killing 10,000 men who were valiant warriors, and again possessed the land.

The name *Ehud* means "union." I believe union or unity is the deliverer of our cities. Like the Israelites in Jericho who did evil in the eyes of the Lord, the Church has sinned. The consequence of their disobedience resulted in their city being overtaken by their enemies. The disobedience of the Church has resulted in the same consequences. Our cities are reaping destruction as the enemy has sent a deluge of drugs, violence, poverty, and hate to infiltrate them.

Our sin is a lack of love. The Word says, "...put on love, which is the perfect bond of unity" (Col. 3:14 NAS). We have treated the command of our Lord, to love one another and be one as He and the Father are one, as optional (see Jn. 17:21).

Obedience is never optional; but because we have treated it as such, we have reaped the consequences of our disobedience. The leadership of various churches in our cities must come together to pray in agreement. We need to pray the double-edged sword called the promises of God for His Church. The devil has gotten fat or grown in influence and power in the cities of our world. But his works will become ineffective and dead as we pray in unison. As the corporate leadership humbly comes together to receive instruction from our head, Jesus Christ, the power of agreement will loose revival in our cities. Consequently, the demonic enemies who seem too formidable for the Church in number and strength, like the 10,000 valiant Moabites, will be routed as the corporate Church follows our leadership.

Paul wrote:

> *His* [God's] *intent was that now, through the church, the manifold wisdom of God should be made known to the rulers and authorities in the heavenly realms, according to His eternal purpose which He accomplished in Christ Jesus our Lord* (Ephesians 3:10-11 NIV).

A by-product of corporate leadership praying is the pouring out of knowledge and wisdom for battle strategy over our cities. From this union, potent ministries and other manifestations will come forth, bringing answers to the cities' problems. The wisdom of God is thereby displayed to the rulers and authorities in the heavenly places. As the corporate Church receives and uses the strategy for the battle, it will set free those held in bondage by the rulers and authorities in the heavenly realm.

DELAND OF MILK AND HONEY—DELAND, FLORIDA

Since the very birth and inception of Deland, Florida, prayer has played a very integral part. At its founding in the 1870's men and women would meet in one location, as one body, regardless of denomination, and pray for the blessing of God and for the city to be founded on godly principles and character. Prior to the coming of the great evangelist D.L. Moody in 1898, the churches met together to pray and seek the face of God for revival and salvation. On the campus of Stetson University later that year, it was noted that only two students were not saved and that prayers were being offered that they would believe. Twenty-five percent of the population attended a meeting with Evangelist Sam Jones in 1898 to pray and hear the Word of God.

It would be in 1994 that these wells would be re-dug and pastors from most denominations would come together to meet for fellowship and prayer for the city. Citywide prayer meetings were called and attended by over 30 various congregations, denominations, and their pastors. Prayers for peace, blessing, healing, salvation, and for the various city leaders were offered. Pastors came together to pray for the city and its leaders in 2000, and over 8,000 one-hour prayer cards were presented to the city leaders. Officials were overwhelmed and grateful. Each of the city gates are being prayed over so that all who enter will be blessed and experience the presence of God and that the peace of God would reign in the city. Crime rates have dropped, the downtown businesses have been rejuvenated (previously one out of three stores were vacant), and the downtown area recently won an award as the top small-town main-street area in the nation.

Last year over 1.4 million hours of prayer were offered for peace, blessing, and salvation over the city, county, state, and nation. Thousands were linked via web cast, radio, cable TV, and satellite during a three-day event called "Shine Florida," which was hosted on the first night in Deland.

This city, as well as others, is experiencing an open heaven, increased salvations, healings, and the favor of God. The local hospital has been purchased by a Christian organization, and now Christ is being exalted, and even the level of care and confidence in the hospital has increased. Lives are being changed as over 40 pastors serve as hospital chaplains to meet the needs of the people who are hospitalized. The local police department for the first time has a paid chaplain, along with area pastors who serve as volunteer chaplains. The city is being prayer-walked house by house and street by street.

The current Lighthouses of Prayer has been relaunched, and almost every person in the city joined a massive Prayer Fair at the local baseball stadium. Prayer was offered up for salvation, healing, financial needs, family healing, and restoration of marriages, as well as for other needs.

What has prayer done? It has resulted in unity among the pastors, peace over the city, decreased crime, increased healings, restoration of families, salvations, favor in the city and with city leaders and officials, as well as requests from the city for involvement and support from the area pastors and churches. In addition, they are experiencing the blessings of God and the anointing that comes as brethren dwell together in unity.

WHO GETS A VISITATION?

Interestingly, the Christmas narrative gives us insight as to why some cities are experiencing a visitation from the Lord. Luke 2:8 says, "And there were in the same country shepherds abiding in the field, keeping watch over their flock by night." An angel visited these shepherds telling of the Christ child born in Bethlehem. These shepherds received a visitation, which led them to greater revelation and a manifestation of God.

The fact that these shepherds were "abiding in the field, keeping watch over their flock by night" characterizes faithfulness and diligence. Perhaps this is the reason why God chose to visit and reveal Himself to them. If that be the case, we have insight regarding who Christ will visit in these last days.

As pastors and shepherds, we should be watching and praying over our flock at night. I remember hearing Francis Frangipane comment on his understanding of his responsibility as the spiritual authority over his flock. In a seminar he stated, "Every night I pray at least a general prayer over the congregation. When I have failed to do so, the results are felt as early as the next morning by some trouble or tragedy that has taken place in the body."

Nearly two decades ago I first met and began working with Dr. Terry Teykl. I will never forget the prayer exercise his church was conducting at that time. Dr. Teykl would have members weekly volunteer to take the membership roster and pray over it alphabetically. Dr. Teykl set the example by praying over a portion of the roster himself. He was a shepherd who watched over the flock by night.

God has used both of these men and has blessed the churches they served as pastors. I commend every pastor to follow their example.

Note in verse 8 that the shepherds (plural) watched over the flock (singular). What if, collectively, the pastors and shepherds of a city would understand their responsibility to the flock in their city? The revelation was for all who would be "shepherds of action."

The shepherds were ready to jointly act on the revelation given. God is a God of purpose. He gives revelation in order for His people to act. The shepherds were obedient to the revelation. Their obedience resulted in them experiencing the manifestation of God on earth, "For unto you is born this day in the city of David a Savior, which is Christ the Lord" (v. 11).

The manifest presence of God is not just for enjoyment, but for our employment. Verse 17 goes on to say, "And when they had seen it, they made known abroad the saying which was told them concerning this child." Verse 20 says, "And the shepherds returned, glorifying and praising God for all the things that they had heard and seen." I would imagine their message was: "We have seen and experienced the Savior, Christ the Lord. He is born and living in the city of David." As leaders jointly act on the revelation given for their cities, they can expect to encounter the manifest presence of God. We are reminded, through these shepherds, that the purpose of God's visitation is to point people to the Savior and Lord who lives in their cities.

> THE MANIFEST PRESENCE OF GOD IS NOT JUST FOR ENJOYMENT, BUT FOR OUR EMPLOYMENT.

The shepherds need to be unified in seeking God's revelation for the Church in their city. God will give His plans to those shepherds who are united to act on the revelation received. God will be manifested in our midst, and many will come to know Christ as living Lord in our cities.

UNIFIED PRAYER

James 5:16 states, "The effectual fervent prayer of a righteous man availeth much." Our prayers avail before God, and then it is God who avails on the earth. As the Church is righteous, meaning as we have a right relationship with God and one another, we, the Church, become like one righteous man in Christ. As one righteous man we can confidently believe that our fervent unified utterances will avail before God, and He will avail much on the earth on our behalf by pouring out the latter rain.

The great revivals in America's history were always preceded by concerted prayer. Historian James Deforest Murch informs us of the pre-revival conditions which took place before the move of the Holy Spirit in the 1800's.

The great revival in America was preceded by concerted prayer. A group of 23 New England ministers, including Stephen Gano of Providence, and Isaac Backus of Middleboro, issued a "Circular Letter" calling the ministers and churches to pray for revival. The Circular Letter contains the following interesting paragraphs:

> To the ministers and churches of every Christian denomination in the United States, [a call] to unite in their endeavors to carry into execution the humble attempt to promote explicit agreement and visible union of God's people in extraordinary prayer for the revival of religion and the advancement of Christ's Kingdom on earth.
>
> In execution of this plan, it is proposed that the ministers and churches of every Christian denomination should be invited to maintain public prayer and praise, accompanied with such instruction from

God's Word, as might be judged proper, on every first Tuesday, of the four quarters of the year, beginning with the first Tuesday of January, 1795, at two o'clock in the afternoon, if the plan of concert should then be ripe for a beginning and so continuing from quarter to quarter, and from year to year, until, the good providence of God prospering our endeavors, we shall obtain the blessings for which we pray.[22]

This letter reveals that they met only four times a year to pray for revival, yet it came. No one would consider this amount of prayer to be too demanding, and many would wonder how such a small effort in prayer could bring revival. The obvious key was that it was united, fervent, and effectual prayer.

CHAPTER 9

God Breathes Through His Body

Once Adam was formed, God breathed on him. With God's breath, Adam became a living being. Before God's breath, Adam had form but he had no function because there was no life.

When God desired to revive Israel, He gave a vision to the prophet Ezekiel of a valley of dry bones. God asked a question that was humanly unanswerable: "Can these bones live?" God brought the skeletal parts together and then put flesh on the bones. The many skeletons with flesh formed a human army. Yet one thing remained—the army had no life, no power. Ezekiel was called to prophesy breath to the bones. As he did so, the once dry bones came to life and became an "exceeding great army" (see Ezekiel 37:1-14).

In the Book of Acts, 120 people formed a united body. They were in one accord and in one place, waiting to be breathed on to be given life, and to become effective imparters of this life (see Acts 2:1-4).

God breathed and gave life to human forms and again He breathed onto His people who, united, formed His Body on earth.

God breathes His life through form. The form takes on life when God breathes.

God breathes life to His Church through prayer. We are talking about the breath when we receive the Holy Spirit. As we form the united Body of Christ in our communities, the Holy Spirit can breathe the breath of revival into His Church. God desires to breathe life into His Church. He is looking for the form. Where God sees that unity, the supernatural breath of revival will be blown upon His Church. You have heard the saying, "Don't waste my breath," meaning "Don't make me talk for no reason." If I speak, I want to be sure my words are heard and acted upon.

God is not going to waste His breath. The Holy Spirit breathes life into forms. The better the form, the more life the Holy Spirit can breathe into it. The better the formation of unity, the greater capacity the Church possesses to inhale the life-giving breath of God and exhale that life into its city.

LEADERSHIP FORMING A UNIFIED BODY

In February 1997, pastors' meetings began to spring up throughout the Tampa Bay, Florida area. Currently, there are seven in various locations. These meetings consist of an hour of worship and prayer. God has rained down His wisdom and given these pastors a covenant of unity. This covenant was signed by 126 pastors on June 10, 1997. Since then, over 250 pastors and ministry leaders have signed it. It continues to be a focal point of helping pastors walk out unity. Many cities throughout the United States, and most recently pastors in Johannesburg, South Africa, have adopted this covenant in whole or in part.

COVENANT OF UNITY

We believe Jesus Christ has one Church, His beloved Bride, for whom He gave Himself. The Church of Jesus Christ in Tampa Bay is comprised of many believers and congregations throughout our communities. Jesus has sanctified and cleansed her with the washing of the

Word of God so that she might be presented to Him, a glorious Church without a spot or wrinkle.

Christ has committed the care, cleansing, and preparation of the Bride to us as shepherds. Endeavoring to keep unity of the Spirit in the bond of peace, we solemnly and joyfully enter into this covenant, pledging that by God's grace we shall:

- Love God with our all, and the Church fervently, doing all things in love.

- Pray for and encourage each other and our congregations on a regular basis.

- Speak well of one another at all times, especially in our preaching and teaching, putting to silence those who would be used by the adversary to spread evil reports among us.

- Hold one another accountable in regard to lifestyle, integrity, and devotional life, meeting together regularly.

- Keep the bond of peace within the Body of Christ by carefully receiving members who have informed their previous church leaders as to their leaving, seeking to resolve any conflict to the best of their ability.

- Be real and transparent with one another, resisting the temptation to impress each other with our size, abilities, or accomplishments.

- Advertise in a manner that is positive for the whole Bride of Christ, and not self-promoting at the expense of other churches or ministries.

- Respect and pursue relationships with those who may be of different distinctives. We are crossing racial and denominational lines, meeting at the cross. We believe in the essentials, unity; in the non-essentials, liberty; and in all things, love.

- Follow the Good Shepherd's example by giving our lives for God's flock in the Tampa Bay Area.

- Prepare the Bride for the return of the Bridegroom, Jesus Christ, by mobilizing our members and promoting area-wide strategies and programs designed to evangelize and impact our communities with the gospel of Jesus Christ.[23]

GOD BREATHES ON THE FORM

After signing the Covenant of Unity, pastors' meetings across the Bay area formed and a prayer/evangelism strategy emerged. God then equipped us with a prayer strategy called "The Year of Answered Prayer." The year of 1998 began with the pastors calling for 40 days of prayer and fasting. We concluded the fast with a unity celebration where the late Dr. Bill Bright of Campus Crusades for Christ was the speaker.

Church members were asked to adopt squared geographical areas called "prayer squares." They were to pray for these assigned areas. Prayer was covering seventy percent of the population of the Greater Tampa Bay area by the end of the year.

God gave us favor with a billboard company, and we were given 20 spaces. As many as 30 calls a day were made as a result of these billboards. Members put out yard signs in their lawns, prayer boxes in businesses, banners on church buildings, bumper stickers on cars; and 250,000 door hangers were distributed. All these tools said to our community, "God's people care and so does God. Need prayer?"

The prayer strategy was so effective that the Billy Graham Crusade adopted it for the crusade in Tampa that October.

God breathed a miracle through the prayers of this unified body. Richard Greene, a local pastor and father of nine children, was getting ready to move his family to South Africa as missionaries. Meanwhile, his oldest son, Ricky, became ill, and tests revealed that he had a cancerous tumor on his brain. Although surgery was performed to remove the tumor, it grew back. A week before Ricky was to go into surgery a second time, our united body in the Tampa Bay area celebrated a second anniversary. Pastors and their members gathered to celebrate what God had accomplished through our unified efforts. The late Bishop Henderson, the United Methodist overseer for the state of Florida, was our guest speaker. He prophetically spoke on the power of the Holy Spirit and asked if anyone needed prayer for healing. Learning about Ricky, the pastors laid hands on him while Bishop Henderson led the prayer. Before the next surgery took place, Pastor Greene felt led to ask the doctors to allow Ricky to undergo another set of tests. The hospital staff reluctantly followed Pastor Greene's wishes. To the surprise of the doctors they could not find the tumor.

Because Ricky had been healed by the Lord, the Greenes continued on with their plan to go to South Africa. Somebody Cares helped open doors for the Greenes to receive support in South Africa, and since then, they have been helping develop teams of church planters in the southern countries of Africa.

The following stories are additional testimonies of how God has breathed through this prayer strategy:

One woman decided to leave early from work with the specific intent of committing suicide at her house before any other family members arrived. On the way home, she saw the "Year of Answered Prayer" banner posted at a local church. She heeded the question "Need prayer?" on the banner and called. The women in the church were immediately dispatched to her house while other intercessors remained on the phone with her. She gave her life to Christ and attended church that evening.

Mary Sullivan would periodically collect the prayer requests for her church from a prayer box she had put in a local supermarket. One weekday she volunteered as the church receptionist and between calls she prayed over the requests that were received.

Praying Up a STORM

While Mary was serving at the church that day, a lady *mistakenly* called the church…or so she thought. The caller said, "I'm sorry. I must have the wrong number." Mary, being an intercessor, was sensitive that the Lord may have arranged this mistaken call. "Are you sure?" Mary asked. They began to converse. The woman eventually gave her name. As she did, Mary looked down at the prayer request slips and saw the exact same name listed on a slip.

"Did you put a prayer request in a red box in the last week or so at a Publix supermarket?" asked Mary. "Well, yes, I did. Why?" came the response. "Because I have your prayer request right in front of me and have been praying for you." Mary had the joy of leading this woman to the Lord.

Many other divine appointments have taken place. Pizza delivery persons seeing the yard signs have requested prayer. People just driving by have literally stopped their vehicles and approached a house with a sign asking, "Is this really a house of prayer? My life is a shambles and I need help."

The Kenneth City Church of the Nazarene also adopted a squared geographical area. After one year, they documented that they had more growth in that one year than in the history of the congregation's existence, and 80 percent of that growth came from their prayer square.

The following year, we continued the Year of Answered Prayer. Through the ministry of Ed Silvoso, we challenged people to become "lighthouses of prayer." As a "lighthouse," a person prays for neighbors on his left, right, and across the street. As we registered 1,500 lighthouses of prayer, a local radio station offered us an hour of time whereby we could connect all these lighthouses together in prayer across the Tampa Bay area as they tune in. Today, the program is aired each weeknight! We truly believe we are praying in a canopy, a cloud covering of God's presence, and the rain is falling.

We also began to mobilize the youth to prayer and servant evangelism. Six hundred youth from three different counties applied daily acts of kindness and prayer in their public schools.

The results have been phenomenal. Not only were youth saved, but also teachers, principals, and parents.

Churches and youth groups in other cities are having their own "40-Day Revolution." Richard Mull coordinated the first outreach through Somebody Cares Tampa Bay, and it has since become a ministry of its own, taking their mission to many cities across the country as "Operation Light Force." Richard shares some of those testimonies:

> On Monday, following the weekend event, Donna Anderson (a new believer) was wearing her War T-shirt and dog tag. Her assignment was to pray in front of the front door of her school. She had decided to anoint the door with her anointing oil and pray alone. A girl who was known for her drug usage approached Donna to make fun of her. The girl asked Donna what she was doing. Donna said she was praying for the school, and that it definitely needed it. The girl laughed and asked Donna if she really believed in that stuff. Donna said she sure did believe in prayer. The conversation ended and both girls headed back to class. Two days later the girl came back up to Donna all excited and wanted to talk to her. She told Donna that what she had said two days ago had really made her start to think. Then last night her mother had invited her to go to church with her, and though this girl never went to church, Donna's words caused her to be interested. The girl consented to go with her mom to church. That night this girl decided to become a Christian. The girl had to find Donna and tell her with excitement about the change God had made.[24]

In another testimony, Richard relates:

> Some students in Haines City had written notes to a Gothic student who flatly rejected all attempts at

kindness and even mocked the Christians in their 40-day quest. After many rejections, this student opened up one day and asked what the verse was that they had shared with him. He began to ask more questions and open up to conversations about the Lord. On the last day of the campaign, this Gothic student came to the youth group's special meeting and bonfire. That night he gave his life to the Lord.[25]

Congregations have adopted a program to pray for policemen and firemen. Others have adopted and are praying for civil authorities. A spark that can help bring the Church together and effectively pray for your community is Steve Hawthorne's *Seek God for the City* booklet. This booklet enables everyone to participate at some level of prayer and covers every subgroup of people. We have unified mini praise and prayer gatherings throughout Tampa Bay to kick off the 40 days. On a local radio station program, various celebrities, mayors, pastors, youth leaders, and business people read Scripture and pray daily to promote the effort.

The radio station WTBN has a range that covers nearly 7.1 million people in a seven-county area. Each Thursday night we are given an hour of free radio to pray. During this hour the radio pastors and business people discuss prayer, share testimonies, and offer effective ways to reach those around us, and then pray.

Each member tunes in and prays for their neighbors in agreement with those leading the prayer in the studio. What awesome potential we have to saturate the entire Bay area on a weekly basis with God's presence being rained down through agreeing prayers.

An AM station may be willing to give the churches in your area a free half hour or hour to unite churches and neighborhoods in breathing the life of God and His blessings into your community.

Ted Haggard writes in his book *Primary Purpose,* "As we pray for our cities, the spiritual climate can be altered as evil spirits are removed and the blessings of God comes. A community that has been prayed for has a much higher response to a gospel presentation than a community that has not received prayer."[26]

In addition to the general prayer covering through these various means, there are also S.W.A.T. teams—God's special forces in Tampa Bay. S.W.A.T. stands for:

S- trategic

W- arfare

A-t

T-ampa Bay

These S.W.A.T. teams usually include ministries that are tackling key locations or people in prayer. Bill and Pam Malone of Pray U.S.A. have had a boat cruise in our bay (the Bay of the Holy Spirit) and prayer walk the bridges that connect our communities in Tampa Bay. "Set free if you want to be" is a group that prays specifically for the homosexuals. Elaina Peters uses a prayer quilt to pray for the pastors in geographical regions throughout the Tampa Bay area. All the various prayers fill up the cloud; God in turn showers our community with blessings. But it won't happen without a fight.

CHAPTER 10

Praying Up a Storm Means War

PRAYING UP A STORM WILL GET YOU THROUGH YOUR STORM

Some storms we encounter are ordained by the enemy. There is an agenda of destruction, despair and discouragement that the enemy sends our way. The problems we often encounter are not merely the troubles we have in this life, but a direct attack because we are children of the King. Therefore, we must fight in the heavenly realms as the apostle Paul instructed us. We do that by praying up a storm.

Implement the principle of displacement that was discussed earlier where we removed the demonic cloud and replaced it with Christ's presence. In order to change your circumstances that the storms ordained by satan brings, you must change the spiritual climate. You'll not just get through the storm of the enemy, but be done with it. You'll not just get through the negative situation, but have God's positive solution as He rains down His will for you life. In other words you'll have His storm that blesses.

Praying Up a STORM

A perfect example of how praying up a storm will get you through a storm was demonstrated by the New Life Church in Colorado Springs, Colorado, whose pastor is Ted Haggard:

PRAYER: COMMUNION AND CONFRONTATION

Shortly after we started the church, I invited a handful of men to pray with me in my basement on a cold winter night. One man in the group—I'll call him Ron—said God was revealing to him that a demonic, religious spirit named Control was at work in our city. He said that the Holy Spirit actually enabled him to see the spirit. Ron sensed that Control was masquerading as a good spirit that had gained authority in several key churches in the area. Now the spirit had come to assume authority over the newly birthed church. We were not about to let that happen. I and the others commanded the evil spirit to bow "in the name of the Lord Jesus Christ." At once I sensed resistance; the spirit was refusing to bow. Ron could "see" the spirit, like the silhouette of a man struggling with an unseen opponent.

We continued to pray. "We command you, in the name of the Lord Jesus Christ, to bow to his Lordship. Because of the cross, because of the blood and because of the Word of God, you must submit to his lordship."

For forty minutes we battled in prayer. "In the name of the Lord Jesus Christ, we announce to you that you will never exercise any control over New Life Church and that you are now forbidden to make any other churches in the city controlling, manipulative or judgmental. You are defeated. Now bow in the name of Jesus!" In an instant we knew that what we had prayed for was accomplished. Ron saw Control fall to its knees. We felt invigorated, relieved and pleased that we had actually engaged and defeated an enemy. But we wondered if this little prayer meeting in the basement of my home might create more conflict with the religious demonic powers in the area.

TANGIBLE RESULTS

Even though weird things were happening, we decided not to talk about them in our Sunday believers meetings or even make an issue of them in our Wednesday night prayer meetings. Instead we increased our commitment to pursue God's plan for our region and talked about His vision for Colorado Springs. We confronted the enemy aggressively in private while denying him unnecessary attention in public.

Our basement church grew in attendance from twenty-five believers to over seventy by the end of April. But we didn't appear to be doing anything right. According to the church growth books, our location, publicity, facilities, printing, parking, staff and finances were wrong—everything was wrong except our hearts. So, just as the four months ended, the Lord faithfully provided a series of miracles that allowed us to move the church from the basement into a public location. In the midst of those miracles and the strange spiritual encounters, we prayed and fasted more. That helped us find the core reason to press on through the opposition and keep taking the risk that someone would even physically harm us. In short, the devil had pushed too far. People had threatened us too much. We articulated our primary purpose: to make it hard to go to hell from Colorado Springs.

God was planting His vision in us—His vision for our city and for Colorado.

On one prayer retreat, I saw in my heart a stadium with thousands of men praising God. Armies of men. On another occasion, I saw a center where people could go to pray and fast and meet exclusively with the Lord. No counselors. No therapists. Just open spaces, beautiful mountains and prayer. On a third occasion, I saw a world prayer center where people were coming from all over the world to pray for global evangelism. In the prayer center, intercessors could go into a sphere with a huge globe to pray for people around the world.

Another vision was of New Life Church, full of people worshipping and praising God, learning the Scriptures in an atmosphere of freedom and security. Then it dawned on me: God has a specific dream for my life, my family, my city and my state. We are to be ambassadors of His dream and co-laborers with Him to fulfill it.[27]

God brought to pass the vision He gave Pastor Haggard. What Pastor Haggard and the New Life Church experienced is exactly what I've shared with you in this book and especially this section. This small congregation removed the demonic presence (cloud) and prayed up God's will given through the vision. As they persisted to fill the cloud, God then rained down His purposes for New Life Church and Colorado Springs.

WAR IN THE HEAVENLY REALMS

Who will control the earth? Heaven or hell? These questions imply a conflict. Therefore, to commit to praying up a storm is a declaration of war on satan and his demons. It means we are serious about taking back the glory that is due to Christ by removing the devil's destructive presence. Be forewarned; expect conflict. Yet, as we persevere, also expect victory. The difference between victory and defeat will be determined by our persistence and insistence that His kingdom come and will be done. Not that certain strategies and techniques of spiritual warfare are not important, but all these come by our relentless pursuit of the Savior and His will being established on the earth. Contrary to many people's thinking, Jesus did not preach on persistence in prayer because of God's reluctance to answer. The Bible says that he will answer speedily to those who cry out day and night (Luke 18:7-8). Satan's resistance towards the realization of God's Kingdom being established on earth through prayer is the reason for Christ teaching on persistent prayer. *Satan perceives the earth as his domain and the Kingdom of God being established as trespassing. Because Jesus knows the conflict of the spiritual kingdoms, He calls us to war in prayer.*

God gave me the privilege of discipling a young man, Wilson Okotie, while I was a missionary in Nigeria. Wilson had been sent to the Ijaw people who live along the southern rivers of Nigeria. They did not have the Bible in their language, but they worshipped angels and a god named Igbesu. Many missionaries had gone before Wilson, but failed in their attempts to plant a church. After three months of prayer and fasting, God gave Wilson favor and three young men had genuinely yielded to Christ.

With these three men, Wilson began praying against Igbesu in all-night prayer. Chief Omamwei, the most influential chief of the village, called for Wilson. The chief's children were dying and he wanted prayer. Wilson told him he would pray, but first he wanted to tell him about the One who would be answering that prayer. Rev. Okotie shared Christ, and Chief Omamwei received Him as Lord. This was a big fish, as the chief personally financed most of the buildings where the people worshipped Igbesu.

Several weeks later, the king of the village guards took Wilson as his captive. He brought Wilson before all the chiefs and accused him of winning people from Igbesu to Christ and disturbing the gods of the village. What a great thing to be accused of! Chief Omamwei stood up and asked the other chiefs, "Which of you would allow your son to be driven from your own village?" All replied, "None of us!" "I have adopted this preacher as my own son. No one can drive him out," Chief

Praying Up a STORM

Omamwei said defiantly. The king agreed to allow Rev. Okotie to stay on the condition he would no longer *lead* prayer against Igbesu.

Consequently, Wilson wisely appointed the chief as the prayer coordinator of the church. The chief, in Wilson's place, led the prayers against Igbesu, until he died at a very old age. The church has been established in the village of Ajakrama and since then four other churches in neighboring villages have been planted. We can expect more of God's Kingdom and blessing to be extended as Wilson and these other new believers continue to pray up a storm over the Ijaw people.

The difference between victory and defeat will be determined by our persistence and insistence that His Kingdom come and will be done. Note that certain strategies and techniques of spiritual warfare are not as important as the relentless pursuit of the Savior and His will being established on the earth.

I remember watching the friendship of professional basketball players Magic Johnson and Isaiah Thomas. During television interviews, they would give a gentleman's kiss on the cheek to express their friendship. Early in the playoffs in the late 1980's, the Los Angeles Lakers (Magic's team) were playing the Detroit Pistons (Isaiah's team). Isaiah was going in for a lay-up when Magic came flying in from the side. Magic's arm, moving like a windmill, came crashing down on Isaiah, who fell to the floor, gashing his head. Blood was streaming down his face.

> WHEN WE STEP ONTO THE COURT CALLED OUR PRAYER CLOSETS, WE ARE CONTESTING SATAN'S RULE.

After the game, a reporter asked Isaiah, "Will this change your relationship with Magic? Will you still be friends?" Isaiah replied, "Absolutely. We are friends off the court, but when we step on the court we are enemies." The Lakers were the reigning champions and Isaiah posed a serious threat. He was seeking to dethrone Magic and the Lakers, and nothing was going to prevent him from giving his maximum effort.

Praying Up a Storm Means War

Satan is the prince of this world. He told Jesus that he could give Him the kingdoms of this world, and Jesus never disputed it. So when we step onto the court called our prayer closets, we are contesting satan's rule. He will resist us with everything he has. He wants the glory of God's creation to serve him, and he will do everything he thinks is necessary to accomplish his goal!

Just as He heard Daniel, God hears us as soon as we lift our voices to Him. The angel informed Daniel that from the very first day, his prayers were heard, but "the prince of the kingdom of Persia withstood" the angel for 21 days (Daniel 10:12-13).

Praying up a storm means engaging in a battle with demonic rulers over our communities. Praying in the cloud of Christ's presence means that our Lord will be glorified, which satan hates. Therefore, satan seeks to resist, slow down, and deter this intrusion of God's will. Although the evil schemer knows he cannot stop it, he still hopes to impede the answers to prayer and discourage us from continuing in prayer.

Even though satan can do nothing against our prayers, he can pull out all the stops to keep us from praying. He wants to keep our prayer life in park, knowing once we get rolling we will be more difficult to stop; and then he is through. God allows the struggle to take place because through it the sinfulness of our hearts is exposed and cleansed. A by-product of spiritual warfare is the purification of our hearts. God will use the conflict to make our hearts pure, unalloyed, and solely for Him. The first battle God wants to win is the one over our hearts.

THE FIRST BATTLE GOD WANTS TO WIN IS THE ONE OVER OUR HEARTS.

The exhortation of Christ found in Matthew 7:7-8 reveals this progression:

> *Ask, and it shall be given you; seek, and ye shall find; knock, and it shall be opened unto you: for every one*

that asketh receiveth; and he that seeketh findeth; and to him that knocketh it shall be opened.

Our initial asking with no apparent answer moves us to seeking. As we seek out God to find reasons for the silence from Heaven, we find them. Often our findings are unpleasant. For example, God may reveal that our prayers are selfish or we have hidden sin. However, with repentance and the surrender of our desires and will to His, we will be ready for knowing. Hearts now single towards God can knock loud and long for His Kingdom to come. "To him that knocketh it shall be opened"(Mt. 7:8). For everyone that asks for the latter rain, and seeks to pray up the cloud of Christ's presence, and knocks until the clouds are open with a downpour, shall get wet.

As we look at six steps in conducting warfare prayer, we find that each step is also in the prayer cycle. Therefore, to commit to praying up a storm is, in fact, engaging in spiritual warfare over our cities.

HOW IS WARFARE PRAYER CONDUCTED?

1. **Prepare** — Put on the armor of God; apply the blood of Jesus for protection. Research your city and church history for information that will help your prayers hit the target…"smart bomb praying."

2. **Submit to God** — James 4:7-10 tells you to resist the devil and he will flee from you. Repent of any sins or attitudes.

3. **Pray the nature of God** — Do not "pray the problem."

4. **Pray His destiny** — Pray in His will for your life and church Acts 4:23-33 is an example of the Church praying in its destiny despite its obstacles.

5. **Pray with authority** — Take authority over these powers of darkness (see Mt. 10:1; Eph. 6:12).

Praying Up a Storm Means War

6. ***Turn the attack*** — Pray to reverse the enemy's attack back on himself in order to glorify Jesus (see Rom. 8:28; Gen. 50:20).[28]

In the book of Esther the people of Israel fasted and prayed for 3 days. The evil that Haman had intended for the Hebrews was turned back on him.

Step one includes researching our cities and churches' histories, in order to discover the sins of the forefathers that are visiting the members today, or that have allowed an oppressive demonic cloud to be over the people. Corporate repentance is needed and then application or confessing of the blood of Jesus will break every curse.

The second step is found in the section on more hindrances. That section, as you remember, emphasized the need to repent and circumcise our hearts to have the authority to see the enemy flee. As we discover the hindrances, we must humbly repent and seek the Lord for the cloud of His presence.

In the earlier sections of forming and filling the cloud of Christ's presence, we noted several ways in which that is done. We fill up the cloud by praying the promises of God. The promises are based on who God is, and who He is reveals what He does. This is similar to step 3 in conducting warfare prayer, "Pray the nature of God." Step 4, "Pray His destiny," means to pray His will for your life and church. We fill the cloud by praying God's Word, which is God's will for your life and church. As Christ forms the clouds, we then fill them by praying His promises and His will.

Step 5 includes praying the cloud of Christ's presence over your city; it is praying in His authority over demonic rulers and the earth.

Finally, it is satan's scheme to keep us in sin so he can rain down his destruction. Praying in the latter rain turns the tables and the attack on our enemy.

The word *hinder* literally means "to cut or interrupt." Satan tries to cut into or interrupt our efforts or attempts to deepen our own prayer life.

He seeks to interrupt any plan to see souls and cities transformed. Now more than ever, we must have a warrior's mentality if we are to keep satan from succeeding in hindering us. Being the army of God must become a reality, not just a metaphor. As in the case of Daniel, God hears us as soon as we lift our voices to Him. The angel informed Daniel that from the very first day, his prayers were heard, but "the prince of the kingdom of Persia withstood" him for 21 days (see Dan. 10:12-13).

In First Thessalonians 2:18, the apostle Paul informed the church at Thessalonica, "For we wanted to come to you—I, Paul, more than once —and yet satan hindered us" (author's paraphrase). If satan could hinder Paul, a church planter and one who suffered to accomplish God's will, then he can and certainly will do all he can to hinder us from praying up a storm.

Chapter 11

Rain for the Nations

Psalm 2:6 tells of the Father enthroning His Son: "But as for Me, I have installed My King upon Zion, My holy mountain" (NAS). Then in verse 8, the Father tells the Son, "Ask of Me, and I will surely give the nations as Your inheritance, and the very ends of the earth as Your possession" (NAS). The fulfilled prophecy about the incarnation of Christ tells us:

> *For a child will be born to us, a son will be given to us; and the government will rest on His shoulders; and His name will be called Wonderful Counselor, Mighty God, Eternal Father, Prince of Peace. There will be no end to the increase of His government or of peace, on the throne of David and over his kingdom* (Isaiah 9:6-7 NAS).

Psalm 86:9-10 agrees with the above Scriptures:

> *All nations whom Thou hast made shall come and worship before Thee, O Lord; and shall glorify Thy name. For Thou art great, and doest wondrous things; Thou art God alone.*

We know that this will be completely fulfilled at the return of Christ where people from every tribe, tongue, and nation will worship Him. Yet, God has called us to see His Kingdom come now, to make disciples of all nations within our generation. It is not to make our name great but to let them know He is the hero of the world. We are seeing this come to pass as we join Jesus and ask for the nations to be submitted under Christ's rulership now.

Uganda was historically known as a people who made covenant with tribal gods through human sacrifice. This cultic practice unleashed a spirit of death and destruction over this lush country. Repressive leadership from Iddi Amin DaDa, Milton Obote, and others left the common man in fear daily. In 1984 imprisonment, torture, and death were assigned to the church through the military; millions died. On top of this, the World Health Organization declared that by 1997, one third of the population would be wiped out through AIDS.

It was this persecution that caused underground prayer meetings to spring up across Uganda. The churches across the nation began to unite in fervent, desperate prayer for God to show up and stop the death and destruction.

One pastor's words clearly reflected his attitude: "If I am to die, let me die seeking Him." Another elderly man provoked the Church to greater intensity when he pointed his cane to the pastor who was praying in a meeting and asked, "Has the God of Uganda gone to sleep? Where is the God of power you preach?"

Churches throughout Uganda began to travail for its country through all-night prayer. The clouds of Christ's presence were formed and being filled. An initial cloudburst took place when Evangelist Robert Kayanja went to plant a church in the city of Kampala. He brought with him six intercessors to Kampala. When he arrived Musoki, a witch doctor, began cursing the young evangelist and team so that they would die. The spirit of death he released for them instead boomeranged and attacked the witch doctor. The notable witch doctor Musoki died; the removal of this conduit for evil allowed Christ's presence to prevail. Authenticated miracles took place in the meetings. The heavens began to open over the Church in Uganda, and it began experiencing a downpour of God's presence.

The presence of God was being felt in every prayer meeting throughout the country. Every zone and every community was praying. Pastor Jackson Senyounga of Christ Life Church went from seven to 2,000 members in a few weeks to a present-day 20,000 plus. Many others are experiencing Day of Pentecost-like expansion. The following are some results from the downpour of God's Spirit on Uganda.

- The crime rate has dropped 50 percent.

- The economy predicted to collapse is now the third fastest growing of African nations.

- Citywide prayer meetings are commonplace where they are thanking God for unity, not asking God for unity.

- The AIDS epidemic is in recession on a national scale, and people with full-blown AIDS are miraculously being healed. One pastor has reported 372 cases cured.

- Many national political leaders are standing for Christ.

- A new ministry of ethics and integrity is established with a believer at its head.

- "Zero" tolerance for corruption has been adopted as a standard for the country.

During the country's 2000 millennium celebration in their national stadium, the president and the first lady read a covenant, which proclaims Uganda as a country committed to the lordship of Jesus Christ for the next 1,000 years.[29] This information about prayer in the nation of Uganda was taken from the *Transformation II* video produced by the Sentinel Group, George Otis Jr., President.

SPRINGS IN THE DESERT

In Zechariah 14:17, God pronounced a judgment, saying

And it shall be, that whoso will not come up of all the families of the earth unto Jerusalem to worship the King, the Lord of hosts, even upon them shall be no rain.

As I thought about this Scripture, the terrain of those nations that lie within the "10/40 window" came to mind. The 10/40 window includes those people who live between 10 degrees latitude and 40 degrees longitude, an area which comprises 2.4 billion unreached people on the earth. The terrain primarily consists of dry desert lands. The 2.4 billion people who live in the window are mostly desert dwellers who have never heard of King Jesus and have never worshipped Him. Most of the countries within the 10/40 window follow Islam. Five times a day, prayers from within the mosque are amplified through the towers, filling the heavenlies with spiritual death. Perhaps this is why they face devastating drought. Again, the physical is often a window to the spiritual. This natural drought speaks of their spiritual barrenness. This satanic cloud looms over them not only to withhold the rain, but to bring a plague of destruction. The Bible speaks of the destruction that will come to those who fail to worship King Jesus.

And it shall be, that whoso will not come up of all the families of the earth unto Jerusalem to worship the King, the Lord of hosts, even upon them shall be no rain. And if the family of Egypt go not up, and come not, that have no rain; there shall be the plague, wherewith the Lord will smite the heathen that come not up to keep the feast of tabernacles (Zechariah 14:17-18).

Of course, we have witnessed the extent to which the horrors of famine, pestilence, natural disasters, and disease have ravaged India, Africa, and parts of Asia. Satan rains down these various forms of destruction, until ultimately, the plague of sin damns these souls to eternal hell.

A spiritual desert exists in our own nation, but is not apparent. The physical drought in Florida is like the spiritual drought in the United States. Florida vegetation gives the appearance that there is no drought. The grass and palm trees look vibrant, and the plants seem green and lush. However, underneath the ground there is a well of water called the aquifer. The aquifer is a reservoir or water reserve that has kept the plants flourishing, giving the false appearance that there is no drought.

The same is true spiritually in America. Financial prosperity in this country appears to mean it is in great shape. But in fact, the society is spiritually shallow. There is no depth. Even Christians who confess to being saved do not actively attend a church. Many polls taken among Christians show their beliefs as a whole do not differ that much from worldly people.

This is a "void." The spiritual aquifer of our society is running on empty. Without rain, Florida's grass will eventually wither and die. Likewise, without the rain of God's presence, America will become a spiritually parched, dry, barren land. Let us pray that revival will come to *fill up* the lives of people to *overflowing* with the love and grace of Jesus Christ.

There is hope! God promises to bring springs in a desert (see Is. 43:19). We need to pray in the cloud of God's presence that will "melt the hearts of the Egyptians." God's promise that His name shall be great among the Gentiles is sure to come to pass. This 10/40 window is the last barrier to its fulfillment. Today, millions of believers are being mobilized to pray for those unreached peoples in the 10/40 window. We are praying in the swift cloud, which the Lord will ride upon. His presence will melt hearts and cause them to throw away their idols, false religions, and pagan traditions (see Is. 19:1). God will rain down His manifest presence through the latter rain. The miraculous work through the outpouring of the Holy Spirit will bring the Muslims, Buddhists, Hindus, and communists to embrace Christ.

Praying Up a STORM

However, first and foremost, it is up to us to pray up a storm and get saturated with the presence of Christ through the outpouring of the Holy Spirit. Our failure to pray cheapens the relationship that was so costly for Jesus Christ to establish. We can offer our quality time and best hours in prayer, but we often don't find God's purposes important enough to do so. Instead, we give our time to other things that become our idols.

Karen Burton Mains, in her book *Making Sundays Special,* includes the story of Elzeard Bouffier. I am passing along this bit of history in hope that it will be a source of hope and encouragement to the nameless servants who are faithful to pray over the vast desert of souls who are perishing within the 10/40 window.

> In an article titled, "The Man Who Planted Trees and Grew Happiness," published in *Friends of Nature,* Jean Giono tells the story of Elzeard Bouffier, a shepherd he met in 1913 in mountain heights unknown to tourists in a region of the Alps thrusting down into Provence, France.
>
> At this time the area was a barren and colorless land where nothing grew but wild lavender. Former villages were now desolate, springs had run dry, and over this high, unsheltered land, the wind blew with unendurable ferocity.
>
> Giono discovered that the shepherd had been planting trees on the wild hillsides. In three years he had planted 100,000 of which 20,000 had sprouted. Of the 20,000, the quiet man expected to lose half to rodents or to the caprice of nature. There remained 10,000 oak trees to grow where nothing had grown before.
>
> Returning to the mountainside after the First World War, Giono discovered a veritable forest and a chain-reaction in creation. The desolation was giving

way to verdant growth; water flowed in the once empty brooks. The wind scattered seeds, and the ecology, sheltered by a leafy roof and bounded to the earth by a mat of spreading roots, became hospitable. Willows, rushes, meadows, gardens, and flowers were birthed. The once desolate villages were once again inhabited.

Officials came to admire this reforestation. A natural forest, they exclaimed, had sprung up spontaneously, none suspecting the precision and dedication of so exceptional a personality as the tree-planter who worked in total solitude, without need for human acclaim. Giono returned again to the region after World War II. Thirty kilometers away from the lines, the shepherd had peacefully continued his work, ignoring the war of 1939 as he had ignored that of 1914. The reformation of land had continued. Eight years later the whole country glowed with health and prosperity.

"On the site of the ruins I had seen in 1913 now stand neat farms....The old streams fed by the rains and snows that the forest conserves are flowing again....Little by little the villages have been rebuilt. People from the plains, where land is costly, have settled here, bringing youth, motion, and the spirit of adventure. Along the roads you meet hearty men and women, boys and girls who understand laughter and have recovered a taste for picnics. Counting the former population, unrecognizable now that they live in comfort, more than 10,000 people owe their happiness to Elzeard Bouffier."

This illustration moves me and stirs me deeply because I believe this is an example of the work of holy people who, unacclaimed and unknown, nevertheless quietly, without adulation, go about persistently digging holes into the stripped and striated, spiritually barren world, planting firm, round acorns, seedlings, and saplings—100,00 at first, 10,000 of which take root and survive. And the holy ones go on planting, planting, planting until spiritual ecology is restored—until all that is sacred blooms, takes hold, spreads, leafs, shelters.

Elzeard Bouffier said,

> Each time I pray, I plant. Each morning office of prayer I observe, each compline, each hour given to intercession, each quieted journey of praise as I walk three and a half miles for exercise, each moment of listening to Him, each recorded word in a prayer journal is a planting session. I join hands with other intercessors, old men and women whose names I do not know, but who are present with me in this spiritual network, planting trees in the wilderness of our world, planting weekly, daily, hourly....[30]

The streams in the deserts of the 10/40 window will flow because of the thousands, if not millions, of unknown, unacclaimed intercessors. These behind-the-scenes warriors consistently send up vapors that eventually become droplets of life poured out by the Spirit upon the Hindus, Buddhists, and Muslims who live in the land. These new converts will become trees of the field, planted by the Lord, bringing eternal life through Jesus. Where there once was only dried, dead religion that left people desolate, the new forest of believers will conserve and produce life that the living waters bring. The tens of thousands of converts will owe their lives to the anonymous intercessors who prayed up a storm.

The *Houston Chronicle* printed an amazing Associated Press story of answered prayer. Eduardo Sierra, a Spanish businessman who was a devout Roman Catholic, stopped to pray at a church during a trip to Stockholm. The church was empty except for a coffin containing a man's remains, so Sierra knelt down and prayed for the deceased for 20 minutes.

Sierra signed the condolence book after he saw a note saying those who prayed for the dead man should enter their name and address. He noticed he was the first to sign. He ended up being the only one to sign.

Several weeks later he got a call from the Swedish capital informing him he was a millionaire. Jens Svenson, the man he had prayed for, was a 73-year-old real estate dealer with no close relatives. He had specified in his will that "whoever prays for my soul gets all my belongings."

The moral of this story could be, "If your prayer of faith doesn't raise the dead, then let it raise a million!" Seriously though, Sierra had no idea or expectation that his prayers would yield him a financial blessing. He acted unselfishly, obediently praying for someone's soul. Even though we don't pray for the dead or a departed soul, the principle of unselfishly, obediently praying for souls who inevitably will one day depart is similar. We may not see the fruit of our prayer of faith until we see the Lord face-to-face. Then will we know the full extent of our prayers' effects and receive unexpected rewards for our prayers of faith. Until then, we must constantly intercede in prayer for others.

Andrew Murray said, "Praying constantly for ourselves will come to failure. Only in intercession for others will our faith, love, and perseverance be aroused and the power of the Spirit, which can fit us for saving men, be found."[31]

The word for "nations" in the New Testament is from the Greek word *ethnos*. We get our word *ethnic* from it. It represents not merely nations but ethnic or people groups who need Christ. According to the U.S. Center for World Missions, 45,000 people around the world join together to pray for a specific unreached people group or a key mission. When people join together to pray for unreached peoples, God's heart is touched because He desires to fulfill that promise of every tribe, tongue, and nation being a part of His Bride. One story illustrates this fact. A missionary on leave told this true story while visiting his home church in Michigan.

> While in Africa, I served in a small field hospital. Part of my duties there involved traveling by bicycle every two weeks to pick up supplies. This was quite a trip though, and took two full days to make, so, midway between the hospital and the town, I would find a place to camp out overnight.
>
> On one of these trips, I stopped by the bank to get some money and then picked up the medicine and supplies that were on my list when I saw two men fighting. By the time I made my way to the center of things, the fight had ended leaving one man on the ground seriously hurt. I treated his injuries and, as I was bandaging him up, I talked to him about Jesus. When I had done all I could and was certain he would be okay, I got on my bike, took my two-day trip and arrived safely back at the hospital, forgetting about the entire episode.
>
> The next month came and again, I did my supply run. When I got back to the city, I was happy to see the young man I had treated, looking much better than he had the last time I saw him.
>
> He seemed to have something important to tell me, so I stopped and sat with him. He told me that while I was taking care of him, he noticed that I was carrying money and medicines with me. He said that in spite of my goodness to him, he and some friends had plotted together to follow me into the jungle and overtake me in the night. "We planned to kill you and take your money and drugs, but just as we went to your camp, we saw that you were surrounded by 26 armed guards."

I was confused as I always traveled alone. I laughed at the notion of being escorted by armed guards. The young man persisted though, insisting that he and his five friends had counted them, before becoming afraid and leaving the campsite.

At this point in the missionary's message, one of the men in the congregation stood up and interrupted. After asking the missionary when this took place, the man in the pew began telling the rest of the story…

On the night this happened to you in Africa, it was morning here and I was getting ready to go play golf. While I was out on the course, I felt a sudden and strong urge to pray for you. In fact, the feeling was so intense that I called others in the church and had them meet with me to pray for you.

He then turned to the congregation and asked all the men who came to pray, to stand up. There were 26.[32]

As small groups led by God's spirit congregate to pray a canopy of His presence will cause His Kingdom to prevail on the earth.

CHAPTER 12

A Canopy of God's Presence

God's desire is not merely to send sectional or regional downpours of His presence, but that "the whole earth is full of His glory" (Is. 6:3). Habakkuk 2:14 states, "For the earth shall be filled with the knowledge of the glory of the Lord, as the waters cover the sea."

As the worldwide prayer movement gains momentum, I believe a spiritual canopy will cover the earth.

Many experts believe that in the beginning there was a massive water vapor canopy that surrounded the earth. Dennis R. Petersen, author of Unlocking the Mysteries of Creation, draws his biblical conclusion of such a vapor existing at one time from Genesis 1:7: "And God made the firmament [or expanse of the sky], and divided the waters which were under the firmament from the waters which were above the firmament…."

Petersen comments, "Could this 'waters above' have been more substantial than the clouds we see now? Perhaps a massive canopy of water vapor surrounding the entire globe was located high in the atmosphere."[33]

Petersen further explains that from a physical viewpoint the idea of a water vapor canopy is not far-fetched because such phenomenon exists around the planet Venus and around Titan, Saturn's moon.

If such a canopy did exist, it would have resulted in no extremes of hot or cold. The rays of the sun would have been evenly distributed causing a continual growing season, no wastelands or deserts, and universal lush vegetation all around the world. With the existence of such a canopy, longer life spans and larger specimens of life could have existed. Of course, this would explain the length of life among those first living on the earth and the enormous size of the dinosaurs.

What was once physically surrounding the earth can now spiritually exist. What was lost by Adam can now be restored spiritually through the second Adam, Jesus Christ, and His Body on the earth. A cloud canopy of God's presence surrounding the earth can now produce spiritually what the water canopy produced physically.

It is interesting that the earth's environment is prophesied through Scripture to bring great decay and destruction (i.e., earthquakes, famine, floods, etc.). Yet, as the physical elements bring chaos, those who are His will have the peace that surpasses all understanding because of the cloud canopy of Christ's presence.

If the cloud of Christ's presence would surround the earth, we would see even distribution of the light of His gospel. We would not see any spiritual wastelands or deserts. The canopy of Christ's presence would produce a continual growing season, Thus we would see believers producing fruit and fruit that would remain. Of course, spiritually the canopy would not produce longer life but eternal life. When you consider that over 170 million prayer warriors are being mobilized through ministries such as AD 2000 and Beyond, Praying Through the 10/40 Window, and numerous others, we have every reason to believe that such a cloud canopy is being prayed up.

In Revelation 14:14-15, the apostle John is seeing the spiritual realities that will take place at the end of the age. Christ is seated on a great cloud canopy that has been prayed up by the saints from which He reaps the harvest. This spiritual cloud canopy will exist to produce fruit that remains in the believer so that they might be reapers of the end-time harvest. Therefore, as the manifest presence of God (latter

A Canopy of God's Presence

rain) is poured out through this great cloud canopy of Christ's presence, we will become the light of the world.

A few months after the attack on our nation by terrorists on September 11, 2001, President Bush was asked by a chaplain in the armed forces how clergy throughout the country could pray for the nation. President Bush responded, "I would ask that pastors across this country would pray a spiritual shield of protection over this country because after we do all we can to protect this country, ultimately our safety is in God's hands" (author's paraphrase). This protection is not needed merely from natural but also spiritual enemies.

Stormie Omartian in her book, *The Power of a Praying Nation*, gives 12 ways to pray for the United States, but many of the points can apply to most other nations. Pray these points to rain down God's will for your nation.

1. Pray for the President and his advisors. You will want to pray for him and his family as you would pray for any person:

    a. Good health.

    b. Physical protection.

    c. Discernment, wisdom.

    d. Courage.

    e. Know and pray for his Cabinet and Advisors.

    f. Pray the President has the right counsel.

2. Pray the same way for all elected officials.

    a. Congressmen (both state and national).

    b. Senators (both state and national).

3. Supreme Court justices and all judges.

4. Pray for the military.

5. Pray for an end to crime and terrorism.

6. Pray for the [moral] and spiritual life of our nation.

7. Pray for a strong economy.

8. Pray for educators, teachers and students. This is for our public school system and universities. Point six [point F] and this point are closely tied. The moral and spiritual condition is being molded by our teachers throughout the country.

9. Pray for national unity. Racial and political divisions can destroy the country. I have lived in Nigeria and seen what division will do as four major tribes and hundreds of others, as well as religious divisions, cripple what should be a prosperous country.

10. Pray for the media—another powerful influence on the moral and spiritual climate of our nation.

11. Pray for the nations of the world. Pray for the removal of evil leadership and that God would ordain the righteous to rule (see Daniel 2:21; Proverbs 16:12).[34]

Isaiah 4:4-6 prophesies of a canopy of glory that will surround God's people. It says,

> *When the Lord has washed away the filth of the daughters of Zion, and purged the bloodshed of Jerusalem from her midst, by the spirit of judgment and the spirit of burning, then the Lord will create over the whole area of Mount Zion and over her assemblies a cloud by day, even smoke, and the brightness of a flaming fire by night; for over all the glory will be a canopy. There will be a shelter to give shade from the heat by day, and refuge and protection from the storm and the rain* (NAS).

Christ will purge His Bride, purifying her from sin. This is the repentance to which I referred earlier. As the Church prays, a canopy of glory

A Canopy of God's Presence

will protect God's people from the storms and rain. The storm and rain refer to satan's destructive forces. This passage is saying that those who will become the holy Bride, separated unto Him, will be protected even as He protected Israel with the pillar of cloud by day and pillar of fire by night. He will shelter them with His cloud of glory. The Church will be shielded as such, in order to grow in His grace, becoming Christ-like.

Another point of Scripture explained by author Dennis Petersen is the Genesis account where Adam and Eve, after sinning, were now aware of their nakedness (see Gen. 3:7). Petersen explains that before the fall, the first couple were clothed in God's spiritual likeness, which was the light of His glory. When God's manifest presence was snuffed out via sin, it was then that they could see their nakedness.

The cloud canopy of Christ's presence enveloping the earth and raining down the manifest presence of God through the Holy Spirit will once again produce the likeness of God's glory on the believer. Speaking of the last days, Daniel said, "Those who have insight will shine brightly like the brightness of the expanse of heaven, and those who lead the many to righteousness, like the stars forever and ever" (Dan. 12:3 NAS). The Word of God tells us, "Arise, shine; for thy light is come, and the glory of the Lord is risen upon thee" (Is. 60:1).

Recall that Moses spent 40 days and nights in the cloud covering Mount Sinai where the glory of the Lord rested. Moses entered the midst of that cloud to receive the revelation of God (see Ex. 24:15-18). When Moses came down from the mountain, his face shone. Moses, after being in the presence of God, radiated the glory of God on his face.

Robert Thompson agrees with a great downpour of glory in these last days:

> The promises of the scripture plus the historical pattern of the outpouring of God's Spirit prompt us to believe during the period of time from Luther until now, that the "Latter Rain" will increase in volume until there is a worldwide downpour of glory.[35]

Praying Up a STORM

The manifest presence of God will be so strong in the last days that others will see a difference because of our character, and like Moses, the literal light of His glory will be manifested on the believer. I'm not saying that everyone will experience this, but I believe we will see it literally manifested on some. All believers will be shining one way or another to the glory of God. Just as the physical cloud canopy caused an even distribution of the sunrays, the canopy of God's presence hovering over the earth will create a spiritual atmosphere for the Lord to manifest worldwide.

This spiritual canopy of God's presence is represented using a bridal canopy of a Jewish wedding. Mike Evans in his book *God Wrestling* teaches:

> "The word *glory* comes from another Hebrew word, *kabod*, which means 'heavy, hanging down,' referring to weightier matters, used in the context of marriage. The *hupah* (bridal canopy) at Jewish weddings is the symbol of this weightiness. There is a point at which Christ and His Body will make supernatural spirit-to-spirit contact and will release God's *kabod* with all its heaviness, majesty, and might."[36]

This canopy of Christ's presence serves as Christ's *hupah* or bridal canopy. It is through this canopy that the spiritual atmosphere will be created worldwide. Through it the Church and Christ's bride will find the grace to get herself ready for the wedding feast of the Lamb. She will be dressed in the glory of her Bridegroom, Jesus Christ.

Romans 8:19-22 states that the world is groaning to see the manifested sons of God. Could Paul have been referring to a time when God's people will literally see manifested on their persons the glory of God, which Adam experienced before his fall?

The world is awaiting the restoration of man to the full image of God, which is to His glorious light. In Frangipane's book *The Days of His Presence*, he says, "I believe that Jesus' disciples were waiting for

A Canopy of God's Presence

the unveiling of His glory, and that this revelation was the compelling motive in their lives."[37]

The glory Frangipane is referring to is not the glory of Christ manifested through His believers in Christ-like fruits and gifts of the Spirit, but the literal light of His glory the disciples saw on our Lord at the Transfiguration.

Author Frangipane answers those who would question the possibilities of the literal splendor or brightness of God's glory resting on us:

> ...the Bible references nearly 400 instances where the glory, splendor, or majesty of the Lord are mentioned.
>
> No one would think it was unscriptural to say that Moses actually beheld God's glory or that the Lord's glory shone from Moses' face. Neither do we debate whether Israel saw God's glory on Mount Sinai or at the temple dedication. Millions of Hebrews saw with their eyes the glory of God. They saw the glory of God rest on a building, a mountain and a man. That same glory is in us now.
>
> In the same way people who are oppressed or demonized can actually exhibit a gloom or darkness in their countenance, so those whose spirits have been filled with Christ will increasingly exhibit His glory as we near the end of age. The idea of the Presence of Christ manifesting in His people by distinguishing light is not foreign to New Testament thought. One only has to observe the paintings of the early masters to see saints with luminous bands of light around their heads.[38]

As God manifests Himself, even to this extent among the Church worldwide, it will bring the end-time harvest, as people will be attracted to His glory.

PRAYING SAINTS AND THE FINAL JUDGMENT

A principle throughout the Bible is that God eventually judges those who have been given a manifested revelation of God and have rejected it, and thus, rejected Him.

God judges us according to our revelation. At first, God's judgment of Moses, prohibiting him from entering the Promised Land for his sin of anger, appears harsh. However, God judged Moses with a higher standard because Moses was privileged to speak to God "face to face, as a man speaketh unto his friend" (Ex. 33:11).

This concept continues with Pharaoh, who, having seen the awesome power of God through the plagues, still refused to let God's people go. God judged Pharaoh and his army when the Red Sea, which had been parted for Israel, closed upon the pursuing Egyptians, drowning them.

In John 9:39 Jesus said, "For judgment I am come into this world, that they which see not might see; and that they which see might be made blind" (see also Mt. 10:14, Mk. 6:11). The initial phrase, "For judgment I am come into this world," is a unique, but accurate one by our Savior. Jesus Christ, God incarnate, was the manifest presence of God on the earth. It was after the self-righteous, religious leaders of Christ's day rejected His presence on earth that judgment came to them and the nation of Israel in 70 A.D.

Another passage we previously noted, Revelation 14:14, is about the great end-time harvest, which I believe comes about from the latter rain and the manifested presence of Christ. If we look at the succeeding verses, we find the great and terrible wrath of God immediately follows. In Revelation 14:16-20, we see the principle of righteous judgment taking place after God clearly reveals Himself and His plans.

From Revelation 8:3-5 we discover that the prayers of the saints initiate the final judgment.

> *And another angel came and stood at the altar, having a golden censer; and there was given unto him much incense, that he should offer it with the prayers of all*

A Canopy of God's Presence

saints upon the golden altar which was before the throne. And the smoke of the incense, which came with the prayers of the saints, ascended up before God out of the angel's hand. And the angel took the censer, and filled it with fire of the altar, and cast it into the earth: and there were voices, and thunderings, and lightnings, and an earthquake.

Let us analyze the sequence of events. The prayers of the saints are poured out on the golden altar, which forms a *cloud* of smoke before the throne of God. Then an angel fills a censer with fire and pours it upon the earth. From this fire come, "voices, and thunderings, and lightnings, and an earthquake" (v. 5).

A possible spiritual interpretation can be made of these physical manifestations. The "thunderings, and lightnings," etc. could represent the miraculous power gifts of the Holy Spirit manifested on the earth. "Voices" could represent prophecy and words of knowledge and wisdom. The others may represent "signs and wonders" which reveal God again as El-Shaddai, the Almighty One.

Even if you don't agree, we must conclude from this Scripture and this entire teaching that the prayers of the saints are the catalyst that begins the end-time events and the final judgment. The judgment on the earth is what follows: "The first angel sounded, and there followed hail and fire mingled with blood, and they were cast upon the earth: and the third part of trees was burnt up, and all green grass was burnt up" (Rev. 8:7). (Verses 8-13 describe more of God's judgment and wrath.)

Of course, we do not pray for God's judgment; but what the Scriptures reveal is that, after God is clearly rejected, judgment follows. So it is in these last days. As we pray in the latter rain, which represents the manifest presence of God, a great end-time harvest will result, succeeded by the final and total judgment by God on the earth. By salvation or by wrath all nations will know the Lord is God!

I believe Revelation 8:3-5 is being fulfilled today as God orchestrates the worldwide prayer movement through His Church. The angel of God is pouring out millions of intercessions for the nations received daily before the throne of God at the golden altar.

The results are the demonstration of God's mighty power on the earth to bring salvation to every people. When this is complete, the Church will be taken up and the wrath of God will come. Keep praying up a storm. The end is near. The Kingdom shall reign over all the earth.

GREAT CLOUD OF WITNESSES

The writer of the Hebrew letter admonishes the Jewish converts to continue in the faith by saying: "Now the just shall live by faith: but if any man draw back, my soul shall have no pleasure in him. But we are not of them who draw back unto perdition; but of them that believe to the saving of the soul (Heb. 10:38-39). The author follows this with examples of fellow Jews, who followed God against all odds, even unto death. This is the great faith chapter of Hebrews 11.

Then, beginning in chapter 12, he refers to the people of faith in the preceding chapter. He states: "Wherefore seeing we also are compassed about with so great a cloud of witnesses, let us lay aside every weight, and the sin which doth so easily beset us, and let us run with patience the race that is set before us" (Heb. 12:1).

Missionary to South Africa Pastor Richard Greene remarks that this cloud of witnesses is not merely metaphoric, but a spiritual reality. The saints that have gone on before us are in the great cloud of Christ's presence. Where else would they be, since to be "absent from the body is to be present with the Lord," and since Christ is seated on the white cloud (see Rev. 14:14).

Remember Moses and Elijah ministered to Jesus in the cloud at the Mount of Transfiguration concerning His ensuing death (see Lk. 9:30-34).

Pastor Greene suggests that the cloud which received Christ (see Acts 1:9) at His ascension was the great cloud of witnesses. He points

A Canopy of God's Presence

out that clouds do not receive, but people receive. The word "receive" could be literally translated to the word "welcome."

I say this to point out that the same cloud of witnesses, which encompassed the believers of the Hebrew letter, encompasses us. My personal belief is that they are overshadowing us with intercessory prayer, particularly, prayers for us to be faithful and to endure to the end, knowing our certain victory. If Jesus lives to make intercession (see Heb. 7:25), the great cloud of witnesses must be doing the same since a disciple is not greater than his master.

If Moses and Elijah were to speak to us from the cloud of witnesses, I believe they would tell us to "have faith in God; pray up the cloud of Christ's presence; persevere until He rains on the earth; reap the end-time harvest for the return of the Lord is at hand and we will soon welcome you to your heavenly home as you are..."

> ...*caught up together with them* [those saints who have died and gone on to be with the Lord joining the great cloud of witnesses] *in the clouds, to meet the Lord in the air: and so shall we ever be with the Lord. Wherefore comfort one another with these words* (1 Thessalonians 4:17-18).

ANSWERING OBJECTIONS

Some might object to this teaching of praying in the cloud of Christ's presence, saying, "The Scripture says, 'Christ is set at the right hand of the Father in the heavenly places' (see Eph. 1:20). Therefore, if He is already set there, how do we pray Him into the heavenly places?" Others might ask, "Isn't that arrogant to think we could pray Christ to the position of heavenly places? Does God need our help? Isn't He all-sufficient?"

Yes, He is all-sufficient and is already set in the heavenly places. And, He already is over every principality, power, might, and dominion. He does not need us to exalt Him.

Though the spiritual reality is that Christ is in the heavenly places and over all things, everyone does not experience the blessing of this reality. However, it seems that this was the Ephesians' experience (see Eph. 1:3). There, Paul admonished the Ephesians to continue to experience the reality of Christ and themselves be seated in heavenly places (see Eph. 2:6).

Though Christ has authority over every evil power, that dominance is not totally realized on earth. His Kingdom has come, but His authority and rule is now and in the future. It seems the element needed to make this more of a reality for our churches, communities, and nations, is for believers to know Christ and His rightful position and pray in the cloud of Christ's presence so His Kingdom's rule can be experienced now and forever.

> *But when this priest* [Jesus] *had offered for all time one sacrifice for sins, He sat down at the right hand of God* [in the heavenly places]. *Since that time He waits for His enemies to be made his footstool, because by one sacrifice He has made perfect forever those who are being made holy* (Hebrews 10:12-14 NIV).

Let me suggest that Christ is not merely biding His time until the end has come to make satan His footstool. I believe He is waiting on those for whom He died and made holy through His blood to take the authority given them and overcome the enemy through Jesus Christ.

A good illustration analogy of how the reality of Christ's victory may not be one's personal experience, can be drawn from World War II. General Wainwright was the only U.S. general taken captive. The Japanese initially took him to the Philippines and later to a remote village in Mongolia. During this time, the United States gained victory; however, General Wainwright's captors kept the news from him, and he remained their prisoner.

General MacArthur ordered a search for General Wainwright, and a lieutenant finally found him. The lieutenant flew in on a helicopter, approached the bamboo cage which held the general, and with a salute, he said, "Sir, we have victory." With the news, General

Wainwright made his way out of the confinement and marched to the enemy commander's office. He kicked open the door. Though frail from his ordeal, he firmly pointed his finger at the officer and said, "My Commander-in-Chief has defeated your Commander-in-Chief, and I'm in charge here now."

The reality was the United States was victorious, but that was not General Wainwright's experience. In the same way, Christ is seated victoriously in the heavenly realms, but there are believers and unbelievers alike who are not experiencing the blessings of this reality.

Many believers are in the dark about the authority they have through Christ's victory at the cross. Until they utilize this power through prayer they can remain in bondage and enslaved by the enemy.

Finally, First John 3:8 says, "...For this purpose the Son of God was manifested, that He might destroy the works of the devil." Christ has destroyed the works of the enemy. Yet, we still see satan powerfully working on earth. Christ gave us all spiritual power to overcome satan's evil works. Jesus will not force His way on the earth; He will only permeate and influence as the Church, through prayer, binds satan's presence. The works of the devil will be made powerless as Christ is manifested in the Church.

Praying in the cloud of Christ's presence says, "Yes, Christ. I agree with the Scriptures that say You are enthroned in the heavenly places, and I pray Your presence and authority be experienced in my community, nation, and world."

Let this short chorus, which is frequently proclaimed in Nigeria, motivate you to pray up a storm until Christ returns for His Church:

It is raining all around me.

I can feel the latter rain.

Dear Lord Jesus, give us more rain.

Until we are wet,

Until we are soaked with the latter rain.

Praying Up a Storm

Study Guide

Chapter 1:

The Destiny of the Church Is at Hand

1. Other than what the author has written, how have you been aware of the worldwide revival of prayer the Lord of Hosts is mobilizing?

2. Do you see signs of prayer revival in the Body of Christ in your city? Explain.

3. How is that revival affecting your local church?

4. How has the information of what the Lord of Hosts is doing affected you and your prayer life?

5. Are you ready to be a part of the global prayer movement that is ushering in the end-time harvest?

Chapter 2:

The Prayer Cycle (Part 1)

THE ELEMENTS

1. The first section of this teaching tells us that true prayer will begin with God. We can only pray prayers that touch Heaven. We need the Son, Jesus Christ, and the Living Water, the Holy Spirit. Ask for grace and supplication, or God's enablement, to pray up a storm. Receive His ability into your life.

2. Reread E.M. Bounds' statement. You are totally dependent on God, Jesus, and the Holy Spirit for effective prayer. However, God has also limited Himself to you and other believers as the source through which that power can be yielded. Share how this privilege and responsibility affects you.

3. This week, begin a daily journal of the promptings you receive from the Lord for you to pray. Evaluate your obedience to His promptings. Ask God to make you sensitive to His promptings to pray. Ask God for more grace to respond to Him. After applying this for several weeks, note the change it has made in your spiritual walk, and document your answers.

THE VAPORS

1. We cannot see or feel the vapors ascending, but it is a fact that they are rising. How does that relate to your faith in the area of prayer?

2. How does the physical reality of God causing vapors to ascend in the atmosphere inspire your faith to pray?

3. At times we do not feel our prayers are very effective or that they are reaching God. When do you most often feel discouraged in prayer?

FORMING THE CLOUDS

1. James 5:17-18 states that Elijah was like yourself (an ordinary person). He prayed by faith, and it stopped raining for three and one-half years. And, by faith Elijah prayed again, and it rained. What does this Scripture say to the believer and his potential to pray up the spiritual cloud of Christ's presence?

2. To build your faith, seek out Scriptures that affirm God as one who hears and answers prayer. Pray them to the Lord.

3. Spend time today listening to what the Spirit has to say about your local church. Write out what you believe the Lord desires to do. Search out various Scriptures that agree and pray them. Follow the same pattern for your community/city and your life/family.

4. The ability to persevere will take faith. Do you believe God wants to pour out the latter rain to reap the end-time harvest? Are you convinced there will be a great end-time harvest? If so, do you also believe it will take a great outpouring of God's manifest presence to see it accomplished?

CHAPTER 3:

Persistent Prayer Fills the Clouds

1. What are the types of prayer given in this section to fill up the cloud?

2. God's will is not always done, mentions Brother Andrew, because the conditions for His will have not yet been prayed into effect. What do you believe is God's will for your local church and the Church in your city?

3. Are you willing to persevere in prayer to see His will accomplished? Try to enlist others to persevere with you in prayer.

CHAPTER 4:

The Prayer Cycle (Part 2)

1. Do you believe it is the time of the latter rain? Why or why not?

2. What does latter rain represent?

3. How does God manifest Himself? How will God manifest Himself?

4. How has God manifested Himself to you? (Remember answered prayer is a manifestation of God.)

5. Has God manifested Himself to your community and city in a special way recently?

6. How do you believe God wants to manifest Himself?

7. Give at least two reasons why God desires to give the latter rain.

8. Is the latter rain a one-time event or an ongoing process? Explain.

9. Review the conditions for revival related to the Pensacola outpouring. Can you see these conditions being met in your church or city? What can you do to initiate that process?

Chapter 5:

Sins That Hinder

1. What sins are holding back the great outpouring in your church, community, nation? Can you identify with them and confess them as even the great men of God did?

2. Check your prayer list during the last month and eliminate those items that are selfish.

3. Write out an unselfish prayer that seeks to glorify God in your community.

4. How does one get prepared to receive the latter rain? Is this a one-time act or attitude of the heart?

5. Do you believe satan has a spiritual cloud of his evil presence over our cities? What evidence of this do you see?

6. How does the acid rain represent the lives and prayers of individuals?

7. How does it aid the purposes of satan?

8. Author Allison comments on how we offer up those polluted prayers. What are they? Are you guilty of this? How can you turn it around?

9. Write an example of a polluted prayer. Write a positive prayer.

Chapter 6:

Prayers That Overcome Hindering Sin

1. According to the Beatitudes, a mourner is one who is sensitive to his own sins and the sins of others. Share how you demonstrate that type of sensitivity?

2. If you have not been a mourner by our definition, how can the way you pray change that?

3. Why do you think a person who has an attitude of mourning over sin and those lost, and being persistent, will move God's heart? Give some Scriptures of biblical examples to support your case.

4. Have you entered into the war in your prayer life, or would your prayer life be considered missing in action?

5. Describe a successful or unsuccessful battle with the enemy. What did you learn?

6. What battle are you fighting today? How are you fairing?

7. What confidence do you have in God that you and those whom you are praying for will be victorious?

8. Rizpah was consistent and persistent. Not many of us are as consistent as we should be, but we can be persistent. We should be persistent in praying over friends, family members, and/or loved ones. Many times you can even use Scripture when praying for these individuals. Try and be persistent in this area and then share the results.

"O, God, take out of their heart the heart of stone and put in the heart of flesh" (see Ezek. 11:19).

"Lord, circumcise their hearts, that they might love You" (see Deut. 30:6).

"Lord, do what You did for Lydia: open their hearts to believe the truth" (see Acts 16:14).

"Dear Holy Spirit, convict them of sin. Don't leave them comfortable in their condition" (see Jn. 16:8).

"Jesus, please orchestrate divine appointments as You did with the Ethiopian eunuch to bring them salvation (see Acts 8:26-40).

"Lord, rebuke and drive away the god of this age who blinds their minds, and open their minds to the glorious light of the gospel of Jesus Christ" (see 2 Cor. 4:4).

"Lord Jesus, send ministering angels to them so they might be prepared to receive the gospel" (see Heb. 1:14).

CHAPTER 7:

Christ's Presence Over Your City

DISPLACING THE DARKNESS

1. Describe the principle of displacement.

2. After reading this section, do you see how this teaching parallels the teachings of Wagner and Frangipane? Comment.

3. What is the key to the great harvest of souls in our cities?

4. Before the Israelites took the city of Jericho, the men were circumcised. What spiritual significance does that have in the spiritual warfare over our cities?

5. What are the plagues sin has brought your city and neighborhood?

6. How can you specifically stand between the living and the dead?

Chapter 8:

Leaders Leading the Way to Revival

CORPORATE LEADERSHIP

1. Is your pastor involved in any pastoral prayer group for your city? If not, pray God would touch his heart to do so. Try giving him this book and other material on corporate prayer.

2. Have you seen the leadership in your city walk out the five steps mentioned in Second Chronicles 5? Which ones?

3. Pray for the pastors of your city. Pray for those corporate meetings that have been established. Pray for the spirit of unity and the bond of peace to prevail.

4. Pray they would have ears to hear what the Lord is saying to their city. Pray that they would know the promises for their area and pray them in.

5. Pray they receive wisdom to carry out God's strategy.

6. Pray for humility and for the attitude that seeks to see Christ exalted in their midst.

7. How have you seen satan get fat (grow in power and influence) in your city? How could unity in prayer make a difference?

8. Do some research on your community. Research its history to find out what you believe is the redemptive purposes for your area. Share it with others and pray it in.

9. Is your church a "Viagra church"? Why or why not? What can you do to see true spiritual vitality grow in your church?

10. Work with others to implement the prayer tools we are implementing in Tampa Bay.

    a. Adopt your neighborhood and begin praying for your neighbors. Get to know them by name, their needs, and believe God for the light of the glorious gospel of Jesus Christ to penetrate their lives.

    b. Adopt a business and pray for the owner or manager and the employees. Consider putting a prayer box at their place of employment. Call us or go to our web site (1-888-561-2273 or www.sctb.org) for more information.

CHAPTER 9:

God Breathes Through His Body

1. Take the Covenant of Unity to your pastor and ask him for his opinion. Ask him to sign a similar one with the pastors in your community.

2. Of the many testimonies shared in this chapter, which is your favorite and why?

3. Can you recall a recent answer to prayer and share it with your group?

4. Can you list any testimonies in your city of where God answered the prayers of the unified Church?

Chapter 10:

Praying Up a Storm Means War

1. The Scriptures bear out that Christ desires to see His Kingdom come to all nations. Have you been praying globally?

2. What nations are you aware of that are spiritual deserts other than the United States? The story of Uganda should inspire hope for our nation. Christ can bring streams to a desert.

3. What is the dominating influence in that country?

4. What is a major city in that country that you can pray for?

5. The word "nations" in the Bible comes from the Greek word *ethnos*. We get our word "ethnic" from this word. Jesus was referring to every tribe or people group in the Great Commission. What people group, if any, has the Lord laid on your heart to pray for?

Chapter 11:

Rain for the Nations

1. What is the difference between victory and defeat?
2. What is satan's strategy against the praying Church?
3. Explain why praying up a storm will bring conflict.
4. Explain what conflicts you have had in pursuing prayer for the lost in your city.
5. Exercise the six steps of conducting spiritual warfare or praying up a storm. Journal your experience in prayer.
6. What are some strategic ways that people can pray?
7. What are some key strategic places and people you need to pray for?

Chapter 12:

A Canopy of God's Presence

1. What would the effects be of a physical vapor canopy covering the earth? What would the effects be of a spiritual canopy covering the earth?

2. If God pours out His Spirit in the last days, could His glory be physically manifested on the believer? What support is there for this idea?

3. Why would it be important for believers in the last days to "shine" with the glory of Jesus?

4. Stormie Omartian lists several different ways to pray for America. I encourage you to pick a different way from this list each day or each week to pray for our nation.

5. By what standard does God judge us? What does this mean to you?

6. What initiates the final judgment?

7. Who are our "witnesses"? What is their role?

For more information on unreached nations and peoples, contact groups such as

A.D. 2000 and Beyond, Adopt-A-People, and Praying Through the 10/40 Window.

These are located in Colorado Springs, Colorado, and at the U.S. Center of World Missions in Pasadena, California.

Praying Up a Storm

Endnotes

1. George Otis, Jr., *Last of the Giants* (Tarry Town, N.Y.: Chosen Books, 1991).

2. Francis Frangipane at Renewal Conference, April 1994, Aldersgate United Methodist Church, College Station, Texas.

3. E.M. Bounds, *Power Through Prayer* (Springdale, PA: Whitaker House, 1982).

4. Dick Eastman, *Change the World School of Prayer Manual* (Mission Hills, CA: Change the World Ministries, 1983).

5. Brother Andrew, *Unlock Your Hidden Prayer Power* (Santa Ana, CA: Open Doors, 1987).

6. Tommy Tenney, *The God Chasers* (Shippensburg, PA: Destiny Image Publishers, 1998) 52.

7. Pastor Blake Lorenz, article featured in Jan./Feb. 2004 edition of *Pray!* Magazine, published by The Navigators, entitled God's Fire Falls.

8 Francis Frangipane, *The Three Battlegrounds,* (Marion, IA: Rivers of Life, 1989), 86.

9. Allison Mare, *The Weapons of Our Warfare,* (England: Sovereign World Pub., 1995).

10. *Ibid.*, 207.

11. Tommy Tenney, *The God Chasers*, 53.

12. Bill Gothard, *The Power of Crying Out,* (Multnomah Publishers, 2002) 61-63.

13. *Mission Frontiers*, June-July 1989, p. 15-16.

14. Tommy Tenney and Thetus Tenney, *How To Be a God Chaser and Kid Chaser,* (Shippensburg, PA: Destiny Image Publishers, 2001) 20.

15. *Ibid.*, 21-22.

16. Francis Frangipane, *Three Battlegrounds.*

17. Ed Silvoso, *Prayer Evangelism,* (Ventura, CA: Regal Books, 2000), 87.

18. Eugene Peterson, *The Message* (Colorado Springs, CO: Navpress, 2002).

19. Stringer, Doug, Turning Point Ministries, personal letter. Nov. 1997.

20. Terry Teykl, at the "City-Wide School of Prayer" Orange County, FL.

21. Story submitted by Joe Brown, Burning Hearts Ministries, Tampa, FL.

22. James Murch, DeFrost, *Christmas Only: A History of the Restoration Movement* (Cincinnati, OH: Standard Publishing Co., 1962).

23. Covenant of Unity written and signed by Tampa Bay pastors.

24. Taken from the website of Operation Lightforce.com. Used by permission.

25. *Ibid.*

26. Ted Haggard, *Primary Purpose* (Lake Mary, FL: Charisma House, 1996), p. 26-28,

27. *Ibid.*

28. Terry Teykl, Advancing the Kingdom teaching syllabus (Renewal Ministries).

29. George Otis, Jr. *Transformation II Video,* The Sentinel Group.

30. Mains, Karen Burton, *Making Sunday Special* (Nashville, TN: Star Song Publishing, 1994).

31. Andrew Murray, p. 130.

32. Lynn Valentine, *Miracles: Stories of God's Grace* (Grand Rapids, MI: Premium Press America, 2002).

33. Dennis R. Peterson, *Unlocking the Mysteries of Creation Vol. 1* (South Lake Tahoe, NV: Creation Resource Foundation), 197.

34. Stormie Omartian, *The Power of a Praying Nation,* (Eugene, OR: Harvest House Publishers, 2002) 95-119.

35. Robert Thompson, *The Feasts of the Lord* (Cedar Rapids, IA: Arrow Publications, 1995).

36. Mike Evans, *God Wrestling* (Grand Rapids, MI: Bethany House Publishers, a division of Baker Book House, 2004), 168.

37. Francis Frangipane, *The Days of His Presence* (Cedar Rapids, IA: Arrow Publications, 1995).

38. *Ibid.*

To Contact Dr. Bernard:

If you would like to schedule Daniel Bernard as a speaker or order other materials and books,

please call:

1-888-561-2273(CARE)

or visit our website:

www.sctb.org.

Additional copies of this book and other book titles from DESTINY IMAGE are available at your local bookstore.

For a bookstore near you, call 1-800-722-6774

Send a request for a catalog to:

Destiny Image®

Destiny Image® Publishers, Inc.
P.O. Box 310
Shippensburg, PA 17257-0310

"Speaking to the Purposes of God for This Generation and for the Generations to Come"

For a complete list of our titles, visit us at www.destinyimage.com